Camouflaged Aggression in Organizations

ALEXANDER ABDENNUR

CAMOUFLAGED AGGRESSION

IN ORGANIZATIONS

A BIMODAL THEORY

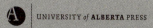

UNIVERSITY *of* ALBERTA PRESS

Published by

University of Alberta Press
1-16 Rutherford Library South
11204 89 Avenue NW
Edmonton, Alberta, Canada T6G 2J4
uap.ualberta.ca

LIBRARY AND ARCHIVES CANADA
CATALOGUING IN PUBLICATION

Title: Camouflaged aggression in
    organizations : a bimodal theory /
    Alexander Abdennur.
Names: Abdennur, Alexander, 1945– author.
Description: Includes bibliographical
    references and index.
Identifiers: Canadiana (print) 20200249037 |
    Canadiana (ebook) 20200249150 |
    ISBN 9781772124910 (softcover) |
    ISBN 9781772125290 (EPUB) |
    ISBN 9781772125306 (Kindle) |
    ISBN 9781772125313 (PDF)
Subjects: LCSH: Violence in the workplace. |
    LCSH: Personnel management.
Classification: LCC HF5549.5.E43 A23 2020 |
    DDC 658.4/73—dc23

First edition, first printing, 2020.
First printed and bound in Canada by
Houghton Boston Printers, Saskatoon,
Saskatchewan.
Copyediting by Anne Laughlin.
Proofreading by Joanne Muzak and
Tanvi Mohile.
Indexing by Adrian Mather.

University of Alberta Press is committed to
protecting our natural environment. As part
of our efforts, this book is printed on Enviro
Paper: it contains 100% post-consumer recy-
cled fibres and is acid- and chlorine-free.

University of Alberta Press gratefully
acknowledges the support received for its
publishing program from the Government
of Canada, the Canada Council for the Arts,
and the Government of Alberta through the
Alberta Media Fund.

Canada   Canada Council   Conseil des Arts
          for the Arts   du Canada

Alberta
Government

CONTENTS

Introduction IX

1 | Three Faces of Aggression 1
Confrontational Aggression, Passive-Aggression, and Camouflaged Aggression

Definition of Aggression   2
Types of Aggression   3
Two Modes of Aggression   4
The Two Modes Are Qualitatively Different   11
The Two Modes Balance and Contain Each Other   14
Modal Shift as an Aggression-Reducing Technique   15
The Implications of the Model for Organizations   17
A Quantum Hypothesis   17
Displacement in Camouflaged Aggression   22
Multidirectional Aggression   24
Resonance of Aggression   25
Warehousing of Aggression   25

2 | A Paradox of Modern Society 27

Bureaucracy   27
Bureaupathology   29
Modifications in Bureaucratic Structuring   31
Organizational Development and Camouflaged Aggression   31

Organizational Complexity 32

Interdependence of High-Tech Systems 33

Antisocial Aggression in Organizations 34

The Strategy of Camouflage 36

The Organizational Person as a Camouflaged Animal 37

A Paradox of Modern Life 39

Phylogenetic Regression 41

Ethical Regression 43

The Convergence on Injustice as a Form of Ethical Decline 48

Incivility as Ethical Decline 50

Machiavellian Management as Ethical Decline 51

3 | Patterns of Camouflaged Aggression 55

1. Indecision 55

2. Rigidity 56

3. Time Manipulation 57

4. Waiting as a Status Degradation Ceremony 59

5. Information Manipulation 59

6. Control by Overwork 62

7. Withdrawal 62

8. Inaccessibility 64

9. Non-interference 65

10. Entrapment 66

11. Random Kindness 66

12. Subordination via Sexualization 67

13. Undermining the Sense of Security 68

14. Ego Bashing 68

15. The Bureaucratic Vendetta 69

The Hydraulic Principle 70

The Hydraulics of Human Aggression 72

The Hydraulics of Camouflaged Aggression 73

Regressive Aggression 76

Self-Destructiveness in Organizations 77

4 | Camouflaged Aggression and Personality   81

Camouflaged Aggression and Personality Disorders   84
Personality Disorders   86
Camouflaged Aggression in "Normal" Personality Profiles   103
Personality Disorders and Voluntary Organizations   110
Personality Disorders and Political Organizations   112
Can Camouflaged Aggression Become Addictive?   113
The Impact of Camouflaged Aggression on Health   114
The Porcupine Entanglement   115
Diagnosing Personality Disorders by Means of a Balance Sheet   116

5 | Sociocultural Factors in Camouflaged Aggression   119

Alienation   119
Anomie   120
Learning and Cultural Transmission   121
Narcissistic Values   122
Cross-Cultural Values and Importation   123
Anti-Confrontation Values   125

6 | Prevention and Control of Camouflaged Aggression   137

Balancing the Two Modes   139
Balancing the Two Modes at the Conceptual Level   140
Confrontation IS the Ideal Strategy   142
Balancing the Two Modes at the Practical Level   144
Intervention Focusing on Abnormal Personality Functioning   151
Other Intervention Strategies   155
Combat Philosophy   162

Epilogue 167

Complexity, Camouflage, Entropy, and Explosive Violence

Complex Systems 168
Camouflaged Aggression as a Complex System 169
Entropy 169
Explosive Violence 170

Glossary 173
References 181
Index 189

INTRODUCTION

THE PURPOSE OF THIS BOOK is to identify common forms and strategies of aggression that are today permeating the workplace and social interaction in general. The expressions of aggression studied here are often carried out in the context of large, complex organizational structures where organizational procedures and regulations can be used as instruments for the delivery of and as masks for the aggression. In this book, aggression is defined as any action or inaction directed by an individual toward the goal of making another individual suffer.

The *bimodal theory of aggression* proposed in this book maintains that when aggression is expressed through formal structures it becomes masked. Four components of the aggressive act can be hidden: the intention to hurt, the perpetrator, the act of aggression, and even the victim. The structures of the formal organization can mask and rationalize all of the above components, while none of them can be masked within a strictly interpersonal conflict. Thus, in the context of formal organizations, the psychological drive of aggression undergoes three qualitative changes: 1) it acquires multiple avenues for expression; 2) it seeks to avoid responsibility or retaliation; and 3) it undergoes a phylogenetically based regression. This regression shares aspects of the camouflage strategy relied on in lower species. The animal uses camouflage (as blending and false pretence) to better zero in on the prey, to escape being preyed on, and to minimize counterattack. The use of camouflage and deception may at certain times be viable in a competitive world; yet it is important to note that humans evolved mainly through directly confronting the world and transforming the environment.

According to the proposed bimodal theory, aggression is expressed through two major modes: the confrontational mode and the non-confrontational mode. These two modes, which emerge from the same drive, become qualitatively differentiated in their social expression and impact. Being qualitatively different, a dialectical relationship develops between them, allowing them to balance and contain each other. Since most types of aggression in organizations are expressed through formal structures, they are often non-confrontational and masked. When avenues for expression and redress belonging to each mode are available, camouflaged aggression is better contained, as this allows the processes of modal balancing to take place. When avenues for the expression of one mode are not available, there is an increase in the aggression in the opposite mode, which is often followed by an increase in the overall level of aggression.

There has been rising public concern about non-violent aggression in the workplace. This type of aggression can negatively impact morale, mental health, and productivity. Four main approaches to workplace aggression have been adopted by experts studying this phenomenon:

1. A *personality* approach, focused on typical personality traits of perpetrators as they behave in organizational settings. Some experts (e.g., Markham, 1993) describe typical cases of "difficult individuals" in the workplace and how to handle them. Others (e.g., Babiak & Hare, 2006) use case illustrations based on the established psychiatric diagnosis in their study of the workplace psychopath. The present study examines the several person-ality disorders in relation to workplace aggression. Established

diagnoses may constitute better reference points than general case studies.

2. A *management* approach, which relates most aggressive behaviour in the workplace to failures in management. Instances of inadequate management create frustrations and conflicts that lead to all forms of aggressive behaviour. Effective organizational behaviour reduces aggression.

3. A *classification* approach, which focuses on categories of abusive behaviour in the workplace. This approach seeks to account for workplace aggression by depicting: 1) the type of aggressive behaviour, 2) the type of harm inflicted, 3) the motive behind the behaviour, and 4) the medium or context of expression, such as physical, verbal, emotional, sexual, and cyber forms of aggression. Such accounts appear under classifications and general constructs such as bullying, mobbing, incivility, abusive supervision, social undermining, work sabotage, and interpersonal conflict. The most popular construct has been *bullying*. The term has been extensively used to refer to forms of behaviour intended to harass, intimidate, dominate, manipulate, and humiliate a person, in the workplace and other social domains (Williams, 2011; Lipinski & Crothers, 2014; deLara, 2016). When bullying is carried out by a group against an individual, it is referred to as *mobbing* (Leymann, 1996; Duffy & Sperry, 2014). An essential assumption for the existence of bullying is an imbalance of physical and social power; the stronger party bullies the weaker. But in complex formal systems the behaviours described as bullying can be carried out without a power differential; they can be carried out horizontally and upwardly through the organizational structure. Accordingly, bullying becomes less distinguishable from conflict where individuals clash over opposing principles, interests, and perceptions. But most importantly, it tends to overlap with other related behaviours, such as abusive supervision, social undermining,

and incivility (Hershcovis, 2011). Paradoxically, the construct of bullying is largely incongruent with the symbol it is attached to. The bull attacks in a straight line and is highly visible, whereas organizational bullying is often indirect and camouflaged.

4. An approach based on *empirical* studies that focus on particular aspects of workplace aggression. These studies seek to conceptualize and operationally define types of antisocial behaviour within suggested working theories and research needs. Articles with this focus started appearing about two decades ago. One well-known book on the subject, *Antisocial Behavior in Organizations* (Giacalone & Greenberg, 1997), dealt with frustration, cognitive dynamics of revenge, determinants of lying, sabotage, whistle-blowing, and organizational culture. This type of research was further expanded as revealed in the contents of a recent book: *Research and Theory on Workplace Aggression* (Bowling & Hershcovis, 2017). This book dealt with topics such as environmental instigators to aggression, improving measurement of workplace aggression, damaging consequences of workplace aggression, perception of abusive supervision, critique of the victim precipitation theory, the role of identity in contextualizing workplace aggression, impact of third-party reactions, spillover of aggression, ostracism as aggression, cross-cultural differences in the reactions to aggression, and coping with and reducing aggression via training and policy interventions.

The growth of research on workplace aggression in the past two decades has been intensive and is moving toward the development of a "scientific" study of workplace aggression. Many antecedents, consequences, mediators, and causal factors have been depicted and analyzed, as indicated by the above list of topics. This progress, in my view, may not be altogether promising, both theoretically and practically, for the following reasons:

1. Most of the topics mentioned above have been already identified in organizational management research that relies heavily on social science theory. The focus of empirical research on aggression limited to the domain of the workplace may narrow the scope of causal relationships in that they lose their larger social context and intellectual relevance.

2. The research findings do not actually contribute beyond what common sense would dictate. The deployment of research methodology or academic sophistication (standard measures, figures, tables, academic jargon, etc.) does not always produce useful knowledge; it may not lead to creative landmarks but rather to rediscovering or relabelling what has long been studied, as in "old wine in new bottles." A research domain can become little more than an arena for the production of publications intended for promotion within academic ranks.

3. The vast number of such papers produced during the last decade are heavily bulked out with references to similar publications. The limited scope and the vast number of cited references from the same context amounts, in my view, to a form of academic ritualism that recycles knowledge and keeps adding to a redundant mass. A fifteen-page article would fetch seven pages of references, most published in the last ten years: this is what qualifies as "fresh" knowledge. The references in the Bowling and Hershcovis (2017) text contain around 1,400 references to articles related to the scientific study of workplace aggression. This proliferation of multidisciplinary research within a specific domain begs the question of its academic and practical value. Such research activity and publishing also constitute a serious threat to the "economy of attention." According to Thorngate (1990), attention is finite in capacity and in operating time. The proliferation of new, often specialized, areas of research in social sciences leads to the compartmentalization of disciplines. The common core knowledge of a discipline recedes, making meaningful and

overarching theorizing scarce. Also, the many new publications may serve, by virtue of their number, to drown out creative contribution. For professionals and students, reading these publications becomes not only a boring exercise, but also an uncertain one; they are read, or partially read, only by those who are writing similar papers. A new academic concern has now arisen: too much researching and publishing and too little reading. We may need to devise ways to reward academics who read published papers as well as those who wilfully desist from publishing!

4. The development of such domain-restricted research in social sciences is doomed to hair-splitting and redundancy. Nietzsche's (1882/1968) theory of eternal recurrence may help explain why there is hardly any way out of this redundancy. The idea of eternal recurrence is a logical outcome of a totally deterministic universe or system. If the parts of a system are finite, then their combinations and the causal links between their parts will keep recurring infinitely. The workplace can be seen as a system consisting of a finite or limited number of relationships that are likely to recur in similar forms. Behaviours such as revenge, sabotage, and status degradation have typical causal antecedents and typical dynamics, despite some variations in the structural setting. These recurring behaviours become readily understandable to experienced managers and administrators with basic knowledge in the social and behavioural sciences. Thus, enlightened management would regard this domain-restricted research and theorizing as superfluous and of marginal importance.

This book identifies constructs and theoretical models that account for certain dynamics of workplace aggression, aggression that is an extension of behaviour that takes place elsewhere in the social and cultural context. The book brings to the organizational context understanding of two universally occurring and challenging developments: *complexity* and *camouflage*. Other concepts are identified and defined, such as modal expression, phylogenetic regression, modal shift, avenues of expression, and hydraulic expression. Major strategies in camouflaged aggression, the role of personality disorders in workplace aggression, and the impact of social values are also discussed. An overarching theoretical relationship (*modal balance*) is advanced. Chapter 1 presents definitions of key concepts and the bimodal theory. Chapter 2 deals with the impact of formal structures and the activation of the strategy of camouflage. Chapter 3 describes the basic patterns of camouflaged aggression and its hydraulic dynamics. Chapter 4 describes the impact of personality disorders on camouflaged aggression, and presents three problematic personality profiles that fall within the range of normal personality functioning. Chapter 5 critically analyzes the sociocultural values that sanction camouflaged aggression. Chapter 6 discusses intervention strategies that are consistent both with the cognitive and managerial-wisdom approaches and with the goal of modal balance. The Epilogue suggests that camouflaged aggression is itself a complex system that can permeate all aspects of society and lead to entropy and disorganization.

The first edition of this book (2000) did well in terms of sales and citations. However, the theoretical model was not critically addressed. I am hoping that the present edition will provoke more discussion about camouflaged aggression, its dynamics, and its social impact. I find a theoretical understanding of camouflaged aggression to be more useful than classifications of injurious behaviour, domain-restricted research, and prescriptive (what to do) approaches. For example, my observations in the area of stress management have led me to believe that individuals who grasped the basic theoretical conception of stress as "excessive demands for adaptation," as originally proposed by Selye (1956), did better in the recognition of stress than those who resorted to detailed lists of stressors and charts of their various impacts. Theoretical understanding helps us to recognize behaviour in its many guises and contexts.

Throughout this text I recommend a *cognitive* approach for the management of workplace aggression. The cognitive approach is defined as one that: a) gives precedence to the appropriate conceptualization of a situation needing intervention, b) views the situation in its broader organizational and cultural context, c) employs theory as an efficient way of understanding the dynamics of the variables involved, and d) considers both micro and macro manifestations and interventions. Above all, this book proposes a challenge to camouflaged aggression by promoting an understanding of its behavioural dynamics, its sociocultural expression, and by endorsing the philosophical position of confrontation.

THREE FACES OF AGGRESSION

*Confrontational Aggression, Passive-Aggression, and
Camouflaged Aggression*

DURING the 1980s and 1990s, the terms "violence" and
"aggression" were used interchangeably to refer to various
overlapping behaviours, attitudes and motivations. This ambi-
guity has allowed many acts of aggression to go unrecognized.
For example, until the end of the twentieth century, most
of the studies on workplace aggression dealt with physical
threats and assaults (e.g., Gapozzoli & McVey, 1966; Kelleher,
1997) while neglecting the more common forms of aggression that are non-violent and camouflaged. There are two
main reasons for this constriction in the use of the term: first,
the term "aggression" has traditionally been applied to behaviour in which an aggressor could be identified (if detected) and
in which the connection between the perpetrator's action and
the victim's injury is apparent; and, second, the term "aggression" has often been used as a synonym for "violence." This was
common during the 1980s, when "aggression" came to refer
only to hostile and injurious physical acts such as war and
physical or sexual assault. The tendency to refer to any and all
forms of injury, coercion, control, or even poverty (Van Soest,
1997), as "violence" may have served as a confusing expansion
of the term. This use also promoted the misconception that
non-physical and passive forms of aggression are less serious

and less problematic than physical and active ones. In current usage "violence" is reserved for physically injurious behaviours, and "aggression" is predominantly used in reference to *any* behaviour which is intentionally harmful. Thus, "violence" should be seen as one form of aggression but by no means the only or most prevalent form.

The first edition of this book (2000), may have had an impact on encouraging the use of aggression as a generic term, and on focusing on its masked forms within the organizational setting. The upsurge of interest in workplace aggression in the past fifteen years has led to the identification of several domains of aggression that were studied under such constructs as bullying, mobbing, incivility, and social undermining. These constructs, as discussed in the Introduction, often overlap, adding more confusion to the concept of aggression and thus compromising proper theoretical analysis. In the last decade experts in the field of workplace aggression appear to be adopting a generic conception of aggression, with a focus on research identifying its consistent expressions. However, this type of research, as discussed in the Introduction, is moving toward domain restriction, which may limit its usefulness, both theoretically and practically.

Definition of Aggression

Arnold Buss (1961) defined aggression as an act or behaviour in which "one individual delivers noxious stimuli to another" (p. 9). Berkowitz (1962) later revised Buss's statement by defining aggression as any behaviour whose intent is to harm. By adding intention, his definition served to correct a problem associated with behavioural definitions such as Buss's, which included unintentional accidents and excluded intentional acts that fail to do harm.

In an attempt to improve on the former definitions, Baron (1977) proposed the following definition: "Aggression is any form of behaviour directed towards the goal of harming or injuring another living being who is motivated to avoid such treatment" (p. 7).

In an attempt to further improve on the foregoing definitions, some authors (e.g., Mummendey, Linneweber, & Loeschper, 1984) have argued that labelling a behaviour as aggression requires taking into consideration the perspectives of the two parties involved in the interaction. They reason that it is necessary to examine both the intentions of the perpetrator and the perceptions and evaluations of the victim. Such authors have added that to be labelled as "aggression" the behaviour must represent a violation of some norm.

Clearly, the perpetrator's and the victim's evaluation of the acceptability of a behaviour may influence the intensity of the behaviour, the reaction to it, and its overall effect. However, behaviour can be injurious regardless of whether or not the perpetrator or the victim believes that the behaviour is acceptable. It also can be injurious regardless of whether either party is aware that the behaviour, or its intention, is harmful or potentially harmful.

Baron's definition, essential to understanding the form of aggression that is the focus of the present book, includes the following aspects of aggression:

1. Aggression involves both intention and potential harm.
2. The intent to aggress may be unconscious.
3. Aggression may involve either action or inaction.
4. Making others suffer can be both a goal and a consequence of aggression.

The following definition will serve the purpose of the present inquiry: *Aggression is any action or inaction directed by an individual toward the conscious or unconscious goal of making other individuals suffer.*

Types of Aggression

Buss (1971) and Berkowitz (1989) have emphasized the fact that aggression can take different forms. Berkowitz labelled two systems of aggression: reactive and instrumental. Buss's classification was similar.

He distinguished between anger aggression and instrumental aggression. The former comprises aggressive behaviour that is motivated by emotion. The latter comprises aggressive behaviour directed toward achieving goals. Buss considered instrumental aggression to be more important and described it as including acts of aggression which could be physical or verbal, active or passive, and direct or indirect.

An important distinction was made by ethologists such as Konrad Lorenz between two levels of causation: the level of motivational sources and that of dynamic expression: purpose versus process. That is, attempts to answer the question "What it is for?" should not be confused with attempts to answer the question "How does it take place?" Lorenz (1966) observed that although goals such as feeding, copulation, and self-preservation may direct an animal's behaviour in a certain direction, they do not fully explain the form that the behaviour takes. The purposeful behaviour of the animal is also influenced by biologically inherited practices, such as ritualized forms of fighting. Similarly, the organizational avenues available for the expression of aggression and their particular dynamics can operationally redefine and mask personal motives such as revenge, lust for power, and jealousy.

The definition of aggressive behaviour adopted in this book endorses the above distinctions but focuses on mode as a central variable in the expression of aggression in organizations. In the expression of aggression within organizations, there is an interaction between the psychological dispositions of the individual and the structural forms of the organization. This interaction assumes a position on a confrontational–non-confrontational continuum or mode, a position that significantly qualifies the expression of aggression.

Two Modes of Aggression

Fundamental to the theoretical model presented in this book is the premise that aggression can be expressed along two opposite modes: confrontational and non-confrontational. The two modes can be expressed through physical, verbal, cognitive, and emotional mediums. Here confrontation is defined as behaviour that is mobilized and focused against some person(s) or issue(s) and is accompanied by declared intention, attendant emotions, and consciousness of values that legitimate the position. Non-confrontation is aggression that is indirect or passive and is often masked by organizational structures. Direct aggression can be part of a non-confrontational strategy (as in the case of challenging a person to avoid confronting an issue, as will be discussed in Chapter 5) and, accordingly, directness may not always be confrontational.

The Confrontational Mode

In the confrontational mode, aggression is expressed manifestly, directly, actively, deliberately, and consciously. For example, if you *physically* assault your supervisors, the act would clearly constitute a confrontational form of aggressive behaviour. It would also be confrontational if you *verbally* criticized them, or rebuked, insulted, or ridiculed them, or if you demeaned them by *non-verbal* facial and bodily expressions of contempt, antagonism, or hostility.

Confrontation brings the social and the psychological components of the aggressive behaviour into conscious awareness; the aggressive activity or methods of delivery are manifest. The author of the aggressive act, its recipient, and the type of injury are identifiable. The intention to aggress and the personal responsibility for it are also easy to discern. Blame can also be attributed. The response to confrontational aggression is often prompt, which makes explicit the conflict that may have engendered the aggression. The often-accompanying anger and hostility help to identify and energize the protagonists. As a result, confrontation may escalate conflict, but at the same time, it may mobilize efforts to resolve it.

The Non-Confrontational Mode of Passive-Aggression

Some social and psychological manifestations of aggression can be suppressed or denied, but aggression will not go away; like a chameleon, it only changes its appearance. We can express our aggressive feelings toward individuals and make them suffer without confronting them or even letting them become aware that we have any such feelings. We can harm them without their knowing that we intended to do so. Such behaviour in interpersonal relations has been labelled *passive-aggressive* (American Psychiatric Association, 1987).

Injuries which are a result of an individual making "unintentional errors" or "forgetting" or "not realizing" or "misplacing" are often a consequence of passive-aggressive behaviour. Loved ones who are "unavoidably" busy or absent when we most need them may be expressing aggression in a passive way which allows them to make us suffer without the necessity of confronting us or acknowledging that they have negative feelings toward us.

A typical example of everyday passive-aggression comes from a study that was reported in the media in the 1980s. The study measured the time it took people to use a public telephone and to pull out of a street parking space. The study found that people took more time on the telephone when there was someone waiting to use it. Similarly, individuals pulling out of a parking space took more time when someone was impatiently waiting to take the space they were proceeding to vacate; they suddenly appeared to become preoccupied with attending to several tasks such as adjusting the seat, the mirror, or the seat belt. Such behaviour is illustrative of passive-aggression employing delay as an instrument of aggression.

I offer another example of passive-aggression, one in which I was the victim. An acquaintance of mine used to engage me in lengthy, detailed, pedantic discourses on certain subjects. In such discussions, when a subject becomes thoroughly covered, participants feel a pressing mental need to draw concluding remarks in order to achieve closure. At this particular point in our discussions, my acquaintance would slip into another topic thus frustrating my quest to reach a conclusion. His cognitive mischief disrupted what the Gestaltists believe is the brain's normal pattern to search for closure.

Aggression is often expressed through inaction. For example, failing to express one's aggressive feelings can create just as much suffering as a loud and clear expression of aggression (a fact to which many spouses can testify). Passive-aggressive behaviour can take many forms, all of which are non-confrontational; they involve actions which convey no obvious negative feelings toward the parties they injure and appear on the surface to be devoid of any hostile intention or malice on the part of the aggressor. Sometimes passive-aggression lies behind obsequious behaviour such as being overly solicitous and apologetic. Many forms of passive-aggressive behaviour in interpersonal relations have stood the test of time and have come to be easily recognized and understood.

However, some non-confrontational aggressors are fully conscious of their aggressive goal while the victim may be totally unaware of it. For example, a common strategy of inmates working in prison kitchens who wish to express their hostility to their guards without running the risk of assaulting them is to urinate in the food which finds its way to the staff dining room. In a technocratic society, a common way to attack people is to infect their computers with viruses or malware. In each of these cases, the intentions of the aggressor are clear but they achieve their goals without having to confront their victim.

Passive-aggression can also be expressed verbally. For example, rather than criticizing someone directly or openly, an individual may indulge in the more common, and less confrontative, practice of spreading malicious gossip about the person among his or her friends. Ross (1999) has referred to such forms of non-confrontational aggression as "interpersonal sabotage."

In the non-confrontational mode of passive-aggression, the perpetrators attempt to mask their aggressive intent and to hide their personal responsibility, sometimes through the use of third parties. However, in many cases the injury is still identifiable and the act of aggression and the perpetrator is readily recognized.

The Non-Confrontational Mode of Camouflaged Aggression

The proliferation of sophisticated technology in formal organizations and everyday life has expanded the avenues for the delivery of aggression. Every newly introduced organizational element, such as the latest technologies, procedures, or regulations, can potentially be used as an instrument of aggression. This situation was eloquently summed up by Al-Mutanabbi, a tenth-century Arab poet: "Whenever nature grows a straight branch, humans attach a spear head to it."*

A formal structure can also be used for masking the aggression. For example, the answering machine and voicemail, while providing a useful service, can be a mechanism to aggress (e.g., through evasiveness) and to mask this aggression. The number of formal structures that can be used for aggression can increase to the extent that aggression becomes difficult to identify and less confrontational. The formal structures provide non-personal mediums for delivery. The development of organizations has enabled and encouraged the expression of aggression to progress to the point where not only the perpetrator and his intention can be masked but the injury experienced by the victim cannot be attributed to the perpetrator and may not even be thought to be a consequence of aggression at all. There may be no identifiable aggression and no identifiable aggressor; both may be hidden, masked, or camouflaged. Victims may attribute their suffering to people or events rather than to their attacker's behaviour. They may blame fate, chance, or circumstances over which they have no control. The aggressor is safe from detection and retaliation from the victim. Victims not only suffer by virtue of the harm they experience but also by virtue of the fact that they feel powerless to respond.

Within organizations individuals no longer need to resolve conflicts among themselves; that is what committees, tribunals, and courts are for. Conflicts between citizens are less likely to be resolved by individuals

---

*كُلَّما أَنْبَتَ الزَّمانُ قَناةً   رَكَّبَ الَمرءُ في القَناةِ سِنانا
المتنبي

openly and directly confronting one another; that has become the responsibility of lawyers. Briefs and motions have become the vehicle for the expression of aggression. Opposing parties are seldom allowed to confront each other even when their squabbles reach open court; their hostility is tempered by procedures, precedents, and manoeuvres that convert the expression of antagonism into legal argument. Antagonists become non-participant observers or mere bystanders in the process.

Mass media also has enormous potential for masking attackers and for blurring the perception of aggressive intent. For example, gossip is no longer limited to our disseminating information to acquaintances; we can readily and anonymously call a reporter to pursue an investigation. Instead of having to take the risk of rebuttal or retaliation against someone whose actions have upset us, we can pass the issue over to reporters who vigorously defend (and seek to define) morality and justice for us. Social media also has huge potential for the aggressive "sharing" of information, false or not, with little or no repercussion.

Organizations afford camouflaged aggression by mediating conflicts through their formal structures and by enabling these structures to be used as weapons and as masks for the delivery of aggression. This phenomenon has caused a transformation in the experience and expression of anger. Anger becomes more suppressed, diminished in intensity, and difficult to invoke. It has come to be replaced by more diffuse and protracted feelings such as dissatisfaction, tension, and resentfulness. As aggression becomes more and more controlled by external and formalized procedures, individuals may come to lose touch with their ability to experience and express anger.

This bureaucratization of anger is consistent with the process of alienation described in the nineteenth century by Feuerbach (1841/1957) and Marx (1844/1964). The essence of this concept of alienation is that parts of human emotions and activity, under certain conditions, come to be experienced in an objectified and externalized manner so that individuals lose their ability to experience these emotions directly and spontaneously. Thus, anger, which is a vital human emotion, becomes alienated and is thus less accessible to the individual. The individual is thereby diminished.

Novaco (1976) has observed that anger serves important psychological and social functions. Anger has an energizing function. Anger facilitates directness in expression and has a self-presentational function of establishing one's identity as a strong and determined person who demands respect and will not tolerate being treated unjustly by others. Anger communicates a commitment to resolving the grievance and orients cognitive processes toward locating blame. The alienation of anger, a natural human emotion, can undermine mental health.

The growth in the number, size, and the complexity of formal organizations has led to the creation of countless structures, rules, and procedures designed to integrate and control the individuals who function within and without the organizations These environments, systems, and technologies simultaneously create opportunities and vehicles for the delivery of camouflaged aggression.

Camouflage and Non-Confrontation

It is important at this point to further clarify the relationship between camouflage and non-confrontation. Non-confrontation characterizes passive-aggression and types of aggression that employ organizational structures in its delivery and its masking. However, there are incidents where aggression employs complex formal structures in a confrontational manner. In this case, the recourse to certain formal procedures is declared, and threats and plans of action are made explicit. Such resort to an explicitly declared strategy removes aggression away from camouflage. It is important to note here that, even in the presence of an intention to confront using organizational structures, the formal structures themselves ultimately impose the non-confrontational mode by virtue of their complexity, timing, and their alienation of procedures. Therefore, camouflaged aggression is, most often, non-confrontational.

Organizational rules, policies, and communication technologies can be employed as weapons, as protective shields, and as smoke screens.

They can be employed to camouflage the following: 1) the act of aggression (e.g., it is budget trimming rather than an act of demotion), 2) the aggressor (e.g., the committee has decided anonymously after deliberations), 3) the aggressive intent (e.g., the termination is part of the need to downsize operations), 4) the injury (e.g., the stress engendered is a part of routine operations), and 5) the victim (e.g., the relocation is a way to increase the employee's experience).

The Two Modes Are Qualitatively Different

Although aggression is delivered through the two modes, *confrontational* and *non-confrontational*, the strategies expressed by them are different in methods of delivery and in impact. This differentiation in the expression of the same drive creates not only qualitative differences between the two modes but also a level of negation and opposition between them. This dialectical relationship becomes central in the management of aggression in organizations, as we shall examine later. The following features summarize the differences between the two modes.

1. The Degree of Visibility of the Aggressive Behaviour

Forms of confrontational aggression are generally easier to identify than forms of non-confrontational aggression from the standpoint of the external observer and the victim. For example, striking someone is more easily identified as aggression than ignoring an injured person. Forms of confrontational aggression such as public slander are more readily identified by the victim than forms of non-confrontative aggression such as malicious gossip.

Forms of confrontational aggression are also easier to identify by the perpetrator. Some non-confrontational aggression can be expressed unconsciously without the perpetrators even being aware of their actions or of their intention to inflict the considerable anxiety and tension that their behaviour can create. An example is the intermittent display and withholding of affection between spouses.

2. The Victim's Ability to Identify the Source of the Aggressive Behaviour

Victims of non-confrontational aggression often find it difficult to determine the source of aggression. For example, in the case of the withdrawal of affection, the victim may self-attribute blame to some aspect of themselves rather than to the manipulations of the perpetrator who has led them to experience anxiety or guilt. Anonymous tips, reviews, and complaints tend to block access to the source of aggression.

3. The Time Taken to Plan the Aggressive Action

The time needed to prepare for non-confrontational aggressive acts is often longer than that needed for direct, confrontational ones. Many acts of non-confrontational aggression require time to conspire. Character assassination, for example, takes more time to achieve than does direct insult.

4. The Time Needed to Carry Out the Aggressive Action

The time taken to express non-confrontational aggressive acts is usually longer than that required for confrontational aggression. For example, it takes less time to interrupt a speaker in order to express one's disagreement than it does to disrupt the speaker by asking frequent and ostensibly valuable but irrelevant questions. Deliberate misunderstanding is a common ploy of the saboteur who, feigning interest, succeeds in making speakers think they are not expressing themselves clearly or that what the speaker is saying makes little sense.

5. The Time Taken for the Injury to Take Effect on the Victim

The time taken for an injury to be experienced is usually longer in the case of non-confrontational aggression. For example, the harm caused by neglect usually takes a longer time to be experienced as abuse compared with the time taken by the victim to recognize the effects of angry outbursts or sudden withdrawal.

6. The Type of Affect That Accompanies the Aggressive Behaviour

While anger and hostility tend to be expressed in the confrontational mode, the absence or the suppression of such emotions tends to be characteristic of non-confrontational aggression. The masking of anger by apologetic and friendly expressions usually accompanies camouflaged aggressive behaviour; anger and hostility are seldom apparent.

7. The Victim's Reaction

Confrontational behaviour is more likely to lead its victims to feel challenged, angry, or hostile, whereas the effects of being subjected to camouflaged aggression are more likely to be somewhat vague feelings of distress, confusion, and depression.

8. Differences in the Likelihood of Conflict Resolution

Confrontational aggression enables conflict to be consciously experienced by both parties. The overt expression may initially heighten the level of conflict, but it often results in release of emotion followed by speedy attempts at resolution. Conversely, non-confrontational aggression delays direct and full-fledged conflict and thus is likely to lead to the prolongation of the conflict and to the perpetuation of hostility, grudges, and vindictiveness (often in a covert form).

In short, there are qualitative differences between the two modes in terms of visibility of aggressive intent, identifying the cause of injury, time expended in planning and executing the attack, time taken to experience injury, accompanying affect, victim's reaction, and the resolution of conflict. These qualitative differences have significant implications for the management of aggression within organizations.

The Two Modes Balance and Contain Each Other

Confrontational and non-confrontational aggression are essentially different expressions of the same drive. Consistent with the dialectical process, differentiated entities create a level of negation or contradiction between them. Accordingly, the two differentiated modes tend to negate and contain each other, or balance each other when avenues for the expression of both modes are available. A high level of the expression of aggression through the confrontational mode can be effectively reduced or contained by a challenge through the non-confrontational mode, and vice versa.

This dialectical relationship may be illustrated in the Freudian position regarding the interaction of erotic sex and affection. Freud (1917/1965) proposes that the erotic-genital expression of sex and that of love-affection stem from the same source (libido). The two differentiated forms of libido are qualitatively different and accordingly tend to negate and constrain each other. For example, the predominance of affection toward children or friends tends to control (repress) erotized expressions. Conversely, heightened genitalized attraction would reduce the resort to sublimated forms of sexual expression.

In settings where the means of expressing confrontative aggression become inaccessible, forms of non-confrontational aggression such as deceit, cunning, legal artifice, and manipulation are likely to soar. Conversely, a lack of legal sanctions or administrative controls on confrontational aggression (or the ineffectiveness of such controls) will allow direct aggression to increase. Sorel (1907/1972) observed that cunning and deceit tend to increase in times of peace and to decrease during violent conflicts and wars. During the early phase (1975–76) of the civil war in Lebanon, which marked the gradual disintegration of the police forces and the arming of civilian groups, it was observed that the behaviour of public servants had suddenly and drastically become civil, polite, and prompt (Atallah, 1976). The empowerment of civilians seemed to have curbed the familiar delaying, callous, and manipulative tactics of the bureaucrats. The strong presence of one mode of aggression can have a containing effect on the other.

The same balancing is also demonstrated in the case of individuals who tend to be fixated at either mode, for instance passive-aggressive individuals and those with explosive rage-prone tempers. Evidence I have gathered from prisons and other institutional settings indicate that individuals who are non-confrontational, such as those with passive-aggressive personality disorders, tend to be most effectively contained by threats belonging to the opposite mode. Confronting passive-aggressives by means of explicit and direct punitive threats tends to curtail their antisocial behaviour. But attempts to counteract the antisocial behaviour of passive-aggressives with strategies involving covert means and bureaucratic manipulation (their preferred approach) appears to be not only ineffective but tends to further stimulate their passive-aggression. Conversely, in the context of a civil war, Masri (1984) documented incidents where the behaviour of individuals in a state of vindictive rage tended to be curtailed or displaced from a target once the possibility of legal accountability became real.

Modal Shift as an Aggression-Reducing Technique

The balancing act of the two modes described above can also be viewed in terms of a deterrent effect each mode has on the other. This relationship can be operationally applied in specific situations as a technique to contain and reduce aggression. An organizational or political group can make a sudden shift to a different modal option to settle a dispute. For example, a call for work stoppage or a street demonstration can push forward a stagnant bureaucratized and legalized dispute. A hostile, boisterous, and unruly reaction to a managerial decision can be promptly contained by referring it to a joint committee for discussion. Thus, modal shifting becomes an important strategy to consider when one is faced with the problem of controlling aggression in organizations. Chapter 6 will elaborate how camouflaged aggression can be curtailed by strategies designed to promote socially acceptable confrontation.

The table below identifies qualitative differences in the expression of aggression along the confrontational and non-confrontational modes.

Confrontational Model	Non-Confrontational Model
I. PHYSICAL MEDIUM	
1. Assault with and on the body (e.g., attempts to hit, push, confine, disrupt a person's activity by means of physical force).	1. Physically injurious behaviour not directly discernible (e.g., through poisoning, indirectly disrupting a person's activity).
2. Assault with the use of a weapon.	2. Placement of objects to allow accidents to happen.
3. Directly risking someone's life.	3. Not giving aid when needed.
4. Taking away or withholding a person's belongings and necessities of life, including nourishment.	4. Sabotaging or losing a person's belongings, "forgetting" to buy food.
5. Terminating an employee with reasons and terms explicitly made clear.	5. Treating an employee in an unsupportive manner until he/she feels ill at ease and leaves.
II. VERBAL-COGNITIVE MEDIUM	
1. Swearing at or direct slandering of a person.	1. Dissemination of information that can harm.
2. Accusation of wrongdoing.	2. Insinuations conveying culpability.
3. Verbal threat to physically hurt.	3. Expressing threat by irony or through a mask of polite speech.
4. Expressing explicitly a certain polemic or biased position.	4. Indirect expression of a position without an explicit assumption of responsibility.
5. Conditional threat to sever communication.	5. Unexpected withdrawal of communication.
6. Disruption of the flow of a conversation.	6. Deliberate misunderstanding and confusion.
III. EMOTIONAL MEDIUM	
1. Anger, hostility.	1. Withdrawal of affect and indifference.
2. Direct rejection (complete severing of affect and communication).	2. Intermittent expression of affect and withdrawal of affect.
3. Explicit threat and inducement of fear.	3. Provocation of guilt and anxiety.
4. Reprimand.	4. Embarrassment.

The Implications of the Model for Organizations

Most organizations are open systems that are constantly subjected to external pressures. In responding to the external and to the internal demands of its sub-systems, each organization strives to maintain a level of equilibrium that allows it to function efficiently with minimal disruption. Although the organization's managers may not be aware of their involvement, the actions they take to achieve equilibrium or system integrity in the organization makes them partners in the management of aggression.

One of the factors which has been understudied is how the organization responds to aggression, and how it generates, directs, and seeks to control the expression of aggression by its members. Managers and researchers alike have been preoccupied with conflicts and their causes within the related personal and organizational parameters, often at the expense of a deeper understanding of the processes of aggression.

A Quantum Hypothesis

The model presented in this book proposes that within all organizations there is an amount or quantity of aggression which differs from organization to organization and fluctuates within each organization, depending on the current strength of a variety of stressors and conflicts, but which is relatively stable over time, and non-reducible to zero. In keeping with the quantum theory in physics, aggression can be conceived to exist in individual units in the same way that matter does, rather than as a constant (e.g., as in electromagnetic waves), and is therefore quantifiable. As a quantity of energy, aggression can be stored and expressed in terms of several processes such as sympathetic nervous system arousal, cognitive-affective attitude, verbal and physical channels of communication, or bureaucratically structured interaction. When avenues for the expression of aggression are available through both confrontational and non-confrontational modes, the amount of aggression within the organization can be maintained at a minimal level by virtue of the above-mentioned balancing and containing process. In other words, the quantity of aggression within a stable organization can be kept (with all things being equal) at a minimal level when aggression is expressed optimally through both confrontational and non-confrontational modes. Thus, the model posits that an unbalanced ratio of expression between the two modes can lead not only to maladaptive expressions of aggression, but also to an increase of the overall quantity of aggression within the organization.

For example, when confrontational aggression in the form of physical and verbal behaviour is condoned and allowed expression without legal or administrative controls, the reaction of many individuals can become extreme as they become less inhibited in expressing direct aggression. As a result, chains of this unimodal aggression may spread throughout the organization as individuals react in retaliation to perceived threats to their physical safety or to their status and dignity. For example, the open exchange of verbal abuse can directly lead to coarse, insulting language, threats, and assault. Similarly, relatively minor physical acts such as pushing or object throwing can rapidly escalate into full-blown assaults or vandalizing. Certain cognitive factors may contribute escalation. A verbal or physical threat may be construed as an insult to dignity, honour, or status, and this interpretation may elicit explosive reactions. Another escalating factor can be displacement. Emotional and verbal aggression may be transferred to others, who consequently perceive this targeting as unjust, and who, in turn, may retaliate. Other catalysing external factors such as personal stressors or political conflicts may also enter the picture. This type of unimodal expressed confrontational aggression is more likely to take place in physically oriented work settings that are undergoing conflicts such as strikes and other labour disputes. Thus, confrontational aggression that is not balanced by avenues belonging to the opposite mode tends to escalate both in terms of range and overall quantity.

The overall quantity of aggression within the organization can also increase as a result of the converse condition in which aggression is expressed almost exclusively through the non-confrontational mode. This increase tends to occur when confrontation is expressly prohibited by norms and institutional controls, while avenues of non-confrontational aggression are lacking such controls. While a unimodal expression augments the spread of aggression, both modes do *not* have the same impact on organizations. Confrontational aggression is more oriented toward escalation and speedy resolution of conflict. It allows immediate catharsis and is not easily displaced on convenient targets, unlike non-confrontational aggression, which spreads, becomes displaced, and eludes direct recognition.

It was noted above that the increase in the quantum of aggression is generated by the interactive dynamics of the two modes and from external pressures acting on the organization as an open system. It should be added that aggression is also fed from the biological reservoirs within the individual. Aggression is continuously generated and stored within individuals and is capable of being deployed within personal interactions—as discussed in Chapter 3.

The dynamic differences between the two modes can be further clarified by a critical assessment of the *heating up and cooling down* model (the "thermodynamics" of revenge), introduced by Bies, Tripp, and Kramer (1997).

According to these authors, revenge (retaliation) cognitions and behaviours follow a pattern of "heating up" and "cooling down." A precipitating event can spark vengeful thoughts and emotions and these can create a heating up process in terms of intensity and duration of affect. This heating up depends on a variety of cognitive, motivational, and social processes that influence how the event is construed. If the heat continues to build, the revenge cognitions and motivation will ultimately find some release: a cool down. Cooling down may follow one of four different paths:

1. *Venting* often involves victims talking heatedly to their coworkers about the harm they sustained (i.e., "blowing-off steam"). Formal

and informal organizational mechanisms for grievance facilitate the venting process.

2. *Dissipation* involves the release of emotional energy without targeted revenge behaviour. Giving the harm-doer the "benefit of the doubt," attributing nonpersonal or external causes to the harm-doer, doing nothing out of fear of retaliation, appealing to rationalizations advocating "don't look back" self-economizing, and actual forgiveness are ways of mitigating and dissipating revenge.

3. *Fatigue* results when revenge cognitions and energy are sustained over long periods of time. Individuals in this condition do not forgive, forget, or "let go." Their rumination about past incidents and regrets about not getting even can become an obsessive preoccupation leading to cynicism and to compromised commitment to the organization.

4. *Explosion* is the expending of built-up energy through an overt and more confrontational retaliation, one which on completion may leave the avenger with reduced desire for further revenge. Explosive acts of revenge can escalate, as in the case of feuding, which can take the form of public complaints designed to humiliate the other party, public demands for apology, "bad-mouthing" the harm-doer, verbal threats of retaliation, blocking the harm-doer's goals, mobilizing opposition to the harm-doer, and, in some cases, even physical violence. The authors also include under this category acts that target the organization, such as employee theft, sabotage, whistle-blowing, and litigation. Other forms of explosive responses include such as meeting privately with the harm-doer, avoiding the harm-doer, and transferring to another department.

The above classificatory model is presented here mainly for the purpose of illustrating the inadequacy of theoretical approaches that attempt to describe reactions to aggression without accounting for the dynamics of its *modal expression*. The mode of expression is tied to the choice of organizational structures and the way these structures are employed in the retaliatory response; accordingly, they can influence the processes of heating up and of cooling down. The non-confrontational strategies of cooling down, such as venting, dissipation, and fatigue, result in minimal draining of aggression, thus allowing it to be stored. On the other hand, a confrontational response directed at the actual perpetrator results in the drainage of aggression, thus minimizing its accumulation.

The impact of the chosen mode can also be demonstrated in the aggressive behaviour of employee sabotage. Clemson (1994) described twelve motivations for sabotage. For instance, employees will engage in sabotage to make a statement, to establish personal worth, to gain revenge, to have an impact in a large bureaucracy, to satisfy a need to destroy, and to vent personal anger created by work-related problems. Sabotage, according to the model proposed in this book, is typically expressed through a covert or non-confrontational mode. Vandalism is more confrontational. If employees are encouraged and given the opportunity to express their anger and hostility openly (i.e., through a confrontational mode), most of the above motives listed by Clemson cease to matter: employees would be more likely to resort to direct alternatives that do not require sabotage. It should be acknowledged, however, that the resort to non-confrontational subversive responses can be unavoidable and, at times, functional, as in cases where the power differential is significant and confrontational action is doomed to fail. However, a focus on modal management would put into a balanced perspective recommendations such as improving security, limiting access, and improving the ability to trace sabotage.

The above "thermodynamic" and sabotage models are more relevant to the non-confrontational camouflaged mode. Non-confrontation encourages the resort to the cooling patterns of venting, dissipation, fatigue, as well as to some of the strategies listed as "explosive," such as sabotage, whistle-blowing, and theft. Despite the relevance of the thermodynamic model to settings that discourage confrontation and direct conflict resolution, it has omitted a major cooling mechanism: that of *displacement*. Not all camouflaged aggression can be contained or expressed through the cooling patterns; a portion of it is displaced. According to the model proposed in this book, displacement of aggression is the mechanism partly responsible for the increase in the quantity of aggression in organizations.

Displacement in Camouflaged Aggression

A fundamental assumption of this proposed model is that there is a qualitative difference between the two modes of aggression. Although displacement can be expressed in the confrontative mode, its expression is containable by the conscious and targetted retaliatory response of the victim. In organizational settings characterized by extensive avenues for the delivery of camouflaged aggression and by the sanctioning of the non-confrontational mode as the only viable and "civilized" mode of expression, instances of displaced aggression are expected to increase. The absence or diminution of the confrontational mode as a normative option, as a structured avenue, and as critical consciousness allow displacement of camouflaged aggression to be delivered spontaneously and sometimes unconsciously using a variety of subtle techniques some of which are discussed in Chapter 3. One employee can displace his aggression onto several interacting employees, and each of the recipients can further displace onto several others. Displaced aggression can increase exponentially, with the result that the overall quantum of aggression may become much greater than it was initially.

The increase in the quantum of aggression within an organization can be illustrated by the following hypothetical case. An executive in a large corporation experiencing what he perceives to be unfair pressure from his board of directors, taking a deep breath, fights to restrain his impulse to tell his board what he thinks of them; he suppresses his anger and acts as though all is well with the world. The blow to his self-esteem creates both anxiety and anger, which he cannot vent against the board for fear of inviting further problems. Unable, or unwilling, to express his anger to the directors, the executive displaces his aggression (by means of various subtle but recognizable negative communications) onto his coworkers or subordinates, who are safer targets. Some of these targets of the executive's aggressive feelings follow suit by displacing their aggression onto their coworkers or subordinates. As a result, the original aggression between the protagonists, spreads insidiously to engender aggression in many other employees within the organization. If the aggressive feelings cannot be expressed within the organization, they may well extend outside, for example, to the victims' families.

Most of us are familiar with the foregoing phenomenon. However, we may not be aware of how its occurrence is a function of the organization's structures, its intolerance of confrontational expression of aggression, and its failure to control displaced non-confrontational aggression.

The notion that "violence begets violence" has become an axiom and most organizations have instituted programs to prevent violence in the workplace. Violent aggression is relatively easy to detect; so is direct confrontation. Accordingly, it is not very difficult to communicate that such expressions of aggression are not condoned and to institute means to prohibit them.

Non-confrontational aggression also begets further aggression. Evidence from studies of interactions in a wide variety of settings (reported in Felson & Tedeschi, 1993) indicate that people generally retaliate against injurious responses directed at them, resulting in a modified "golden rule": *do unto others what they have recently done unto you.*

I have observed that modern organizations have added a couple of qualifications to the above rule. First, *retaliation should be similar in quality.* The response to camouflaged aggression is usually carried out by means of camouflaged aggression and this stylistic choice is dictated not only by the mode of the aggressive stimulant but also by the vast availability of avenues enabling camouflage. Second, *retaliation need not be confined to the perpetrator*; it can be redirected to others.

An alternative approach that our hypothetical executive might have taken to his conflict with his board would have been to identify and objectively evaluate the board's treatment of him, communicate his position to the board, and then confront them by criticizing their conduct in a clear and civil manner. He could use a variety of confrontative strategies in reacting to their behaviour by expressing his discontent while he clarifies his position in terms of how their behaviour impacts both him and the organization. Confrontation need not involve rudeness, insult, or belligerence. He may not win. His self-esteem may not be bolstered by victory. But at least his self-esteem and integrity will not have been jeopardized in knowing that his behaviour was both weak and dishonest. Moreover, he will have acted fairly because his anger was directed at the source of his injury rather than somewhere it does not belong.

There are three main reasons why the executive might wish to avoid confrontation. First, individuals in power may interpret confrontation as a personal challenge and may retaliate in ways which jeopardize the executive's future. Second, many of us have an exaggerated and unrealistic conception of the detrimental consequences of confrontation, and this paranoia tends to increase within bureaucracies as a result of regression to the state of camouflage, as will be discussed in the next chapter. Third, confrontation has come to be viewed as uncivilized and inappropriate behaviour within organizations and the myth has been established that confrontation is possible only for those who have power and are not afraid to use—or lose—it.

Multidirectional Aggression

Although recipients of displaced aggression, in turn, often displace their aggression downward to individuals who are even less likely than themselves to retaliate directly, they may also express aggression toward those above them. The expression of aggression in an upward direction is likely to be even more camouflaged than that which flows downward. For example, subordinates may overload their superiors with information in seemingly sincere attempts to keep them informed, or can "gum up the works" by zealously ensuring that individuals follow the rules and procedures that the superiors established. The term "bureaucratic sabotage" can be used to describe such retaliatory camouflaged aggression. Aggression may also be expressed horizontally to peers and colleagues. Thus, aggression can become increasingly pervasive within the organization.

Resonance of Aggression

During the displacement process, aggression may increase in quantum leaps. Displaced aggression can flare up when it comes in contact with those with certain personality vulnerabilities and disorders, or when an individual becomes the recipient of aggression from multiple sources. For example, upon experiencing displaced aggression consistent with a "conspiratorial" interpretation, an individual with some paranoid characteristics may react with a drastic counterattack of hostility and/or engage in malicious intrigue. Similarly, displacement of camouflaged aggression onto individuals already exposed to much of the same from other sources may result in a last straw-breaking situation, leading to a flare-up of an array of aggressive displacements such as intentional neglect, sabotage, provocation, and avoidant behaviour.

Such sudden escalations or quantum leaps of aggression resemble the phenomenon of *resonance* in physics. "Resonance" refers to a condition in which a vibrating physical system responds with maximum amplitude when it is subjected to a periodic force of the same frequency as its own natural frequency of vibration (Lord, 1986). Various forms of displaced aggression travelling throughout the organization are likely to have particular effects on certain individuals who, owing to their personal idiosyncrasies, amplify them and cause aggression to resonate with more intensity.

Warehousing of Aggression

There is a third factor responsible for increased aggression within organizations. This is the slow process of cathartic release, which is characteristic of non-confrontational aggression. Non-confrontational aggression represents a highly controlled expression of aggression, one which, by virtue of anger suppression and delay of retaliation, is unlikely to fully drain an individual's store of aggression. Accordingly, aggression accumulates in psychological dispositions and in available structural avenues, and can become warehoused as potential aggression.

Although this potential aggression may not be directly observable, it can be readily felt. The feeling of tension and depression that we experience when we step into such settings (despite their often-placid façades) testify to this warehousing of unexpressed aggression. This possibility motivates speculation as to whether conditions such as sick building syndrome, characterized by chronic fatigue, mild depression, and respiratory ailments, may in part be the result of a toxic psychological atmosphere. The physical symptoms may represent kinetic forms of the pent-up aggressive potential.

Warehousing of aggression can be seen as having both structural and psychological reservoirs. Organizations continuously create new conditions, which can render some employees vulnerable to other employees who use these conditions against them. Frequently, the intention to aggress is provoked by the structural opportunity: Why are you harassing them? Because I can. Aggression can also accumulate in the psyche of a person as a result of repeated victimization; it becomes stored as nervous tension that seeks eventual release. Thus, an organization can be seen as a warehouse of potential aggression, as shown in its ability to generate organizational conditions and psychological states that render employees vulnerable.

A PARADOX OF MODERN SOCIETY

ORGANIZATIONS, WHETHER BIG OR SMALL, direct our behaviour through their goals, policies, and structures, and by the social climate, customs, manners, and values they promote and maintain. They have the ability to shape our interactions within the organization and influence our attitudes, values, and behaviour outside of the organization. Organizations are a major source of progress, productivity, and well-being as well as of frustration, conflict, and misery. They control our lives and shape our interests, beliefs, and values. They define our humanity.

Bureaucracy

Most large organizations are structured into some form of bureaucracy. A bureaucracy is a system of organization and management in which roles and tasks are specialized, relationships among people and positions are controlled by rules, and functions are managed within a hierarchical structure. Although the term has become associated with government, red tape, and officialdom, bureaucracy is a normal, logical, and, some would argue, essential development of large-scale enterprise. Weber (1947) views bureaucracy as an organizational structure designed to provide maximum efficiency through the optimal application of rationality. The model bureaucracy involves a group of people operating under normalized, specified standards of activity and output. These division of labour and coordination functions make up the organizational structure.

A fundamental, but seldom articulated, rule in bureaucratic organizations is that the job or position of employment belongs to the organization and not to the individual who holds the position. The employee is not allowed to use his/her position for personal ends. The employee's power is defined and limited by assigned authority. The effective functioning and integrity of an organization can be severely compromised by employees who break this rule and use their positions for personal or material gain. Most organizations have instituted procedures to detect and prevent such transgressions by means of various auditing and surveillance techniques and sanctions. The use of one's position in the workplace for the expression of aggression has been the subject of increasing attention in recent years (e.g., see Abdennur, 2000; see also sources listed in the Introduction in this volume). Employees can use the structures of the organization to express aggression for the purpose of realizing personal ends and needs, both healthy and unhealthy ones. Aggression as a destructive activity needs to be addressed as a managerial challenge. Workplace aggression has been classified according to several categories such as interpersonal conflict, social undermining, bullying, mobbing, and incivility. As suggested in the Introduction, this proliferation of constructs did help to improve identification of aggressive behaviour and has stimulated empirical research; however, this domain-centredness has hindered the development of wider and more integrated theoretical approaches. The first edition of this book (2000) sought to qualify forms of aggressive behaviour on the basis of more generalized variables pertaining to mode and to camouflage. These variables are addressed more fully in this edition; a deeper understanding of them can alter our perception, as well as our management, of workplace aggression.

Bureaupathology

Bureaucracy can bring rationality, predictability, stability, and efficiency to an enterprise. However, the manner in which bureaucracies operate can be highly dysfunctional. Thompson (1961) used the term "bureaupathology" to describe the dysfunctions of bureaucracy. Common dysfunctions of bureaucracies include:

1. Compulsive rule-following and rule-enforcing, which reduces efficiency and creates the mistaken belief that procedures serve as instruments of moral conduct or substitutes for good judgment.
2. Displacement of the organization's service or productivity objectives to the sole objective of maintaining the organization.
3. Conflict between "bureaus," e.g., professionals vs. administrators; workers vs. managers.
4. Hoarding of authority by individuals, which renders others impotent and engenders envy and power struggles.
5. Delay in decision-making.
6. Bureaucratic obstruction, in which employees retaliate against superiors by using the bureaucracy's procedures to block action.
7. Avoidance of responsibility by bureaucrats who shift responsibility to other individuals or offices.

Bennis (1966) has suggested that bureaucracies are frequently prone to the following problems:

1. Inhibiting personal growth and the development of mature personalities.
2. Promoting conformity rather than individual creativity.
3. Failing to take into account the "informal organization," and, therefore, failing to anticipate problems.
4. Thwarting innovative ideas because of inadequate or distorted communication between hierarchical divisions.
5. Producing impersonality which leads to depersonalization.

6. Conditioning individuals so that they become "organization persons" who are overly conforming, dull, and uncreative.

Over the past few decades many writers and practitioners have voiced their dissatisfaction with classical bureaucratic organization and with the impersonality of large bureaucracies. This discontent is reflected in the widespread appeal of a host of best-selling books whose basic theme is that organizations need to be more flexible and to promote continuous learning and adaptation. Perhaps the best-known examples are *In Search of Excellence: Lessons from America's Best-Run Companies* (Peters & Waterman, 1982), *Reengineering the Corporation* (Hammer & Champy, 1993); and *Antifragile* (Taleb, 2012).

On the other hand, some researchers have defended bureaucracy. Perrow (1979), for example, criticizes the extensive preoccupation with "humanizing" bureaucracies and argued that organizations would function well and evolve in a healthy manner without such refinements if bureaucratic principles are adhered to. Robbins (1985), concludes that bureaucracy works regardless of changes in technology and environment and is still effective in a wide range of organized activities. Daft (1989) observes that bureaucracy is the most efficient form of organization available and that it will continue, despite some transformations, to be the dominant form of organization in the foreseeable future.

The problems attributed to bureaupathology are minuscule compared with those associated with organizational and procedural failings. Bribery, kickbacks, influence peddling, and power mongering are behaviours that undermine the competence of organizations. Such dysfunctional behaviours represent failures to implement or maintain the fundamental bureaucratic rule which stipulates that the office belongs to the organization and ultimately to society, not to the incumbent. Many underdeveloped countries actually suffer from a lack of organization rather than from what is often labelled as "corruption."

Modifications in Bureaucratic Structuring

The impact of information technology, advanced technology, diver-
sification, and globalization are leading to qualitative changes in the
functioning of organizations. Luthans (1995) has drawn attention to the
following trends:

1. Organizations are "downsizing" as technology makes it possible to
   do more work with less people.
2. Traditional hierarchical structures are "flattening," giving way to a
   variety of horizontal organizational forms. Networks of specialists
   and decentralized units and branches with increased autonomy
   are examples.
3. The number of intermediary levels of management are in decline,
   and the consolidation and concentration of control are made
   possible by means of information technology.
4. Technicians, or knowledge workers, are replacing manufacturing
   operatives as the worker elite.
5. Organizations are becoming "learning environments" in which
   work activity is being redefined to include constant learning, more
   high-order thinking and a reduction of routine tasks.
6. The paradigm of doing business is shifting from product-making
   to service-providing, with emphasis on continuous redesigning of
   operations to achieve quality improvements.

Organizational Development and Camouflaged Aggression

The changes outlined above indicate a general trend toward decentralization, more administrative autonomy of branches, more reliance on
teamwork, more participation in decision-making, and more empowerment to experts and unit heads. At first glance, these trends might
be thought to promote the reduction of camouflaged aggression since
they involve the reduction of middle management and the facilitation
of access to information. Unfortunately, however, there is little room for

optimism because advanced technology, downsizing, decentralization, and teamwork may have little impact on the reduction of organizational *formalization*. Formalization refers to the process in which organizations standardize behaviour through rules, procedures, formal training, and other related mechanisms. Employees working in a particular unit of a large organization may be less subject to pyramidal hierarchy and thus may enjoy direct, informal, interpersonal contact with colleagues and superiors, but their work lives will still be regulated and controlled by the formal structures of the parent organization. Formalized policies and procedures will continue to regulate and control the daily operations of their work, their income, their promotion, their vacation, and their retirement.

Organizational Complexity

The contemporary organization is a complex system. A complex system can be defined as a large network of components that operate as a whole. There are distinctive properties that can be ascribed to the whole and not to any of the individual parts, and these are referred as the emergent functions of a system (Mitchell, 2009). Advanced technology can simplify work procedures and save time, but it can also introduce new, complex structures. These structures can be used as tools for the delivery of camouflaged aggression and can, by virtue of their technological complexity and their interaction with system-emergent functions, increase the possibility that aggression will be expressed in more subtle and masked forms. For example, a resentful employee may deliberately cause much confusion, frustration, and distress by tampering with an organization's software systems. The same effect can be engendered by the incompetence of an employee dealing with the same complex technology. Therefore, identifying the actual cause of the dysfunctional behaviour becomes a new managerial challenge.

It should be noted in this context that technically advanced systems can reduce certain forms of corruption and related conflicts that take place via direct human interaction and exchanges. Automated systems process information and procedures in a uniform, non-personal manner that often reduces the possibility of fraud, bribery, or preferential treatment. Unfortunately, however, if the antisocial intention persists, corruption will re-emerge in more sophisticated and camouflaged forms.

Advanced technology has also increased the number of positions within an organization whose incumbents have opportunities to engage in effective camouflaged aggression. In classical pyramidical organizations we would expect the quantity and the impact of camouflaged aggression to increase with the elevation of rank. A high rank can provide more access to avenues for the delivery of camouflaged aggression, often through the use of intermediaries. However, the advent of organizational "flattening" and advanced technology has enabled junior or low-ranking employees to engage in camouflaged aggression. Advanced technology may have made organizations more integrated but it has also made them more vulnerable to acts of deliberate mischief. For example, a junior employee working in data entry can put the whole organization into a state of chaos by engaging in software-related mischief. Private information belonging to individuals, corporations, or government agencies can be hacked. A cyberattack can disable vital operations within organizations. A security guard can keep the entire staff locked out by "forgetting" to deactivate an electronic alarm system.

Interdependence of High-Tech Systems

Advanced technology increases the complexity of local systems and the interdependency of these systems further increases the complexity of social interaction. Information technology, for example, links many organizations together and at the same time formalizes their interaction. Interdependence of complex systems is permeating society. Ever-increasing demands are being made on small businesses and individuals to operate in accordance with the rules and procedures imposed by the larger organizations. Procedural complexity is likewise permeating society and all aspects of modern life as organizations grow and specialize. Parsons (1951) predicted that the growth of organizations would lead to the bureaucratization of society as a whole; society itself has become a bureaucracy. Formalized rules for the management of large systems, together with the protocols of information technology, have infiltrated virtually all of our daily activities.

Even taking a vacation has become very complex. Packing the car and driving off to a cottage or campground used to be a relatively individualistic, simple task compared to the preparation for a typical contemporary vacation. Planning a vacation nowadays often involves dealing with a dizzying array of factors such as negotiating vacation time with one's employer, family, and peers; selecting a destination; examining timetables; analysing various types of accommodation, tour packages, pricing restrictions, taxes, insurance, and the like; and reading the fine print of non-refundable contracts. All of these require that we engage in complex decision-making, but our decisions are limited and controlled by formal organizations that make the rules, organizations with which we seldom interact except through an electronic device.

Bureaucratic organizations are often invisible to us and we may not even be allowed to access them except through some intermediary, but their regulations shape our decisions and ultimately take away our power. It is not only the complexity of myriad rules that distresses us, it is also the manner in which those rules are applied by individuals who use them not for the benefit of the organization but to satisfy their own needs, to exert their power, and to express their aggression. The organizational structures and procedures provide them with a vehicle.

Antisocial Aggression in Organizations

It has been stated that corporate organization is "for the white-collar criminal what the gun or knife is for the common criminal—a tool to obtain money from victims" (Wheeler & Rothman, 1982, p. 1,404).

As we shall see, a position within an organization can be a tool not only for financial crime but for crimes against the person. Incumbents can use their position within the formal structure and use the formal structure itself (its rules, regulations, and procedures) as weapons with which they deliver aggression. Their aggression is a special type of anti-social behaviour, not one which we normally associate with crime, but one which is much more prevalent, socially destructive, and deserving of our attention and our censure. It is a type of aggression that cannot be committed outside of an organizational setting.

The organization brings perpetrators and their victims together and provides the perpetrators with both the opportunity and the tools for their antisocial acts. The organization also allows victims to become perpetrators. It creates an ideal setting for the expression of aggression because it relies on clearly defined and legitimized positions of personal power. These enable individuals to control others for their own purposes under the guise of fulfilling their assigned duties. While appearing to operate in the best interests of the organization, one can harm others with impunity. This form of antisocial behaviour is sometimes condemned and at other times is condoned and perceived as prosocial. Many of these techniques are not readily recognizable as aggressive; some are skilfully masked. However, some are more obvious. Most of us recognize the deception of the manager who conducts an exit interview with an employee he has never liked; apologizing profusely, the manager talks about fiscal restraint and personal anguish about its effects on staff, and extols the qualities the employee can bring to another organization which will better appreciate his or her skills. The real reasons for terminating the employee may be entirely personal or non-organizational, but the manager, in conveying their decision to the employee, avoids having to deal with the anger their decision will spawn by cloaking the real reasons behind a veneer of apology, sympathy, and flattery. However, many techniques of camouflaged aggression are not so obvious and many individuals are simply unaware that they are victims or even perpetrators.

Camouflaged aggression has two main characteristics: it is *deceptive* and it enables perpetrators to *avoid responsibility* for their actions. Avoidance of responsibility is often a self-protective measure aimed at preventing or minimizing retaliation. Deception is the active elaboration of basic forms of false pretence. In his book *By the Grace of Guile*, Rue (1994) proposes a working definition of deception:

> Deception occurs when a discrepancy between appearance and reality can be attributed in part to the causal influence of another organism. That is, a deceiver is an organism (A) whose agency contributes by design to the ignorance or delusion of another organism (B). Self-deception may be said to occur when A and B are the same organism. (p. 88)

Organizations provide many avenues for deception, and the complexity of modern organizations has made deceit into an art form. While many individuals do not realize that they are engaging in it, others consider it a sport.

The Strategy of Camouflage

Camouflaged aggression involving non-confrontation and deception has been used throughout history as a way of expressing aggression while avoiding threats to personal safety and survival. When we think of camouflage we must go beyond its use in military practice. Camouflage strategies are used in human interactions where we want our true emotions or intentions to be hidden.

Many forms of camouflage are employed by animals, birds, fish, and insects. In fact, in most species, camouflage is a crucial strategy for survival. Camouflage in the animal world seeks to achieve concealment by way of altering or obscuring appearance and blending with the environment.

Camouflage in animals can serve three functions:

1. *Protecting the animal from being detected by a predator.* This evasive and purely passive function can be observed in insect species. For example, some leaf-eating worms take on the colour

and shape of the leaf to avoid detection by birds. Some moth caterpillars take on the shape and colour of bird droppings in order to avoid being observed and eaten by birds. More active forms of evasive behaviour can be observed when an organism is faced with danger. Some birds fluff their feathers to appear larger and intimidating; some animals feign injury and some play dead.

2. *Facilitating efficient delivery of aggression for predation.* Camouflage increases the ability of a predator to surprise and catch its prey. For example, the chameleon's blending with the grass helps it to go unnoticed as it sticks out its tongue and catches unsuspecting flies. The fox's coat blending with the dried grass helps the fox to hide and surprise its prey.

3. *Protecting the predator from the defensive reaction of its prey.* Camouflage, by giving the predator the advantage of timing and surprise, allows it to catch its victim by surprise and deliver an incapacitating or fatal bite before its presence is noticed. Thus, the predator may be spared the potential injury coming from its prey, as in a retaliatory kick, horn thrust, or a desperate bite.

The Organizational Person as a Camouflaged Animal

Aggression expressed through organizational structures has three essential characteristics:

1. It is usually non-confrontational.
2. It is masked (deceptive).
3. It seeks to enable the perpetrator to avoid responsibility and retaliation.

Camouflaged aggression by organizational incumbents has the same essential features as the camouflage strategies of most animal species. Just as the animal uses its environment to conceal its actions, presence, or intent, an individual occupying a position in a complex organization can use the available rules, regulations, and formal procedures to engage in camouflaged aggression with minimal risk of detection and possible retaliation.

The organizational predator utilizes the same three strategies of camouflage employed by insects, birds, and animals:

1. The organizational predator can "blend" with the formal structures of the organization so as to disappear as an individual entity. A strong personal presence tends to project that one owns responsibility for decisions which impact other individuals. However, it is always possible for bureaucrats to avoid being seen as powerful (and therefore suspect) by hiding their decision-making responsibility. The tenure of bureaucrats who allow themselves to be seen as powerful is often short. Many minimize their vulnerability by burying their identity in committee deliberations where their personal motives can be hidden from view, and any actions they take are likely to be attributed to the committee and not to them personally.

2. Organizational predators often facilitate aggressive behaviour by selectively providing access to sensitive information about certain people. Bureaucracies obtain and store a wealth of information about their members, information which they believe they must have in order to justify the decisions they take about them. Knowledge is power. Information can enable aggressors to identify vulnerabilities in their intended victims and to know where and when to attack without recrimination. The bureaucrat's position offers the advantages of access and timing. Thus, bureaucrats may have access to their victim's file; they may have knowledge about who makes decisions about the victim and information or a position that enables them to influence that person; they may possess information about such matters as schedules and deadlines, which they can use to ensure the appropriate timing for the delivery of their camouflaged aggression.

3. The formal organizational structures protect individuals from direct retaliatory response because their hierarchies limit access

and their structures dilute and obscure responsibility. Disgruntled employees or clients may not know what took place, who made the decisions, who ordered the action, or who took the action, or why. Decisions may simply reach them "through channels." They may feel the teeth piercing them but be unable to identify the animal who attacked them. Without an identifiable perpetrator, victims can only vent their spleen against the organization or even themselves. Attacking an amorphous institution is likely to yield only frustration. Victims will have little success in attributing personal responsibility and hence blame. Without the ability to attribute blame it is difficult to retaliate or justify retaliation. Besides, most organizations have established controls to protect the organization and members of management from retaliation.

A Paradox of Modern Life

The similarity drawn between camouflaged behaviour in human organizations and that in other domains of the biological world is not a mere analogy. Camouflage has been a central strategy in the behaviour of all living species: from the simplest forms of life to the most evolved. For example, some viruses can alter their external shape to mimic certain body proteins and thus escape being detected and destroyed by the immune system of the host. Humans have not abandoned camouflage; it is employed in almost all forms of social interaction that seek deception and manipulation. But throughout their evolution humans have gradually relied more on confrontation and less on camouflage in social interaction. It is the confrontational strategy that accelerated evolutionary trends from mere adaptation to the active transformation of the environment, both physical and social.

Physical forms of camouflage were gradually abandoned as humans and society acquired skills and tools which enabled them to defend themselves without having to hide. The sense of security provided by forming primitive social associations emancipated humans. It enabled them to come out of their caves and escape from their perpetual preoccupation with protecting themselves from predators. Having achieved security in numbers they were able to become more open in their hunting and warfare techniques. Camouflage tactics of course remain part of the operations of warfare; however, the primary strategy in war is confrontation.

Confrontational aggression has been celebrated and idealized throughout history. Many of societies' heroes are warriors. Moreover, many of our cultural symbols express the value of confrontation. The lion and the eagle may have enjoyed such grand symbolic status not only because of their strength and prowess but also because they symbolize active aggression rather than passivity, cunning, and stealth. We admire in them their freedom from preoccupation with self-defence. The lion sleeps twenty hours a day on his belly without the need to protect it; the eagle takes no cover as it perches on the highest branch.

The invention of gunpowder and guns further enriched the symbolic repertoire of confrontation. The gun in itself is a symbol of confrontation. The gun "speaks loud and clear," "means what it says," and shoots in a straight line. Only an assassin needs a silencer. Just before the development of effective long-range weapons around the early nineteenth century, soldiers usually marched into battle in highly visible formations wearing decorative uniforms—the negation of camouflage. At the cultural level, values of confrontation have, until recently, customarily been held in higher esteem than those of cunning and trickery.

The organizational bureaucrat is a modern symbol of camouflaged power, and it is ironic that, although we may aspire to their positions, we may feel contempt for many of them, because we have come to view them as manipulative, deceitful, treacherous, and weak. Many bureaucrats who hold secure positions behave in an insecure manner as they avoid taking unequivocal and open positions on issues, and are prone to ambivalence, procrastination, and indecisiveness. They behave like the camouflaged animal which reacts to any movement in its environment as a potential threat that invokes a "freeze" or "play dead" defensive reaction. Bureaucrats may lose our respect when it becomes clear that the positions they are willing to take on controversial matters are limited to those which do not threaten the status quo. We may recognize that they are motivated by their need to achieve personal invulnerability (and thus perceived omnipotence); they acquire it by blending with the organization so that their identity is obfuscated and therefore safe. Techniques for flushing out such incumbents and moving them from this state of blended omnipotence toward personal accountability will be presented in Chapter 6.

A fascinating paradox appears to be unfolding in the organizational behaviour of post-industrial societies. This paradox represents a confluence and a functional adaptation between one of the most advanced structures of contemporary society (the formal organization) and one of the most phylogenetically primitive strategies: camouflage. Modern organizations are unwittingly resurrecting archaic forms of expressing aggression. The complex systems of contemporary organization are providing a social "foliage" in which the chameleons, the snakes, and spiders among us (and in us) take cover as they prepare to strike. Camouflage is becoming an essential adaptation technique in the most advanced elements of contemporary society.

Phylogenetic Regression

Regression is generally defined as a movement backward; for our purposes here, it means a return to earlier or less mature behaviours or earlier or less mature levels of the organization of behaviour. In psychoanalysis regression is one of the defence mechanisms in which the individual, faced with an anxiety or conflict, returns to a stage or to a behaviour that in the past was advantageous and safe (Wolman, 1973). Freud (1920/1958) likened the process of regression to an army which has left some of its troops at rear bases and, in the face of a strong enemy, retreats to those previously established bases at the rear.

The study of the ancestral succession constituting the evolutionary development of characteristics within a species involves identifying and tracing what ethologists refer to as "homologies"—similar patterns among species that result from their common ancestry. Lorenz (1981) has observed that forms of behaviour can evolve over time in very much the same way as physical structures do. Homologies of structure are fairly easy to recognize from the anatomical study of fossils. Behavioural homologies can be sought only in living species; a judgment of behavioural homology is more complex and requires confirmation of a variety of indicants, but there is little question that behavioural homologies occur.

According to ethologists (e.g., Eibl-Eibesfeldt, 1989), living systems owe their behaviour at least in part to processes of adaptation through natural selection. In evolutionary terms, variants brought about by genetic changes are tested as to their adaptiveness and the genotypes for adaptive traits are retained. This evolution by phylogenetic adaptation is supplemented by adaptation via learning and individual experience and, in humans, via traditions.

Camouflaged behaviour is found in almost every living species. In humans, forms of camouflage have been largely abandoned with the evolution of society and under normative pressures that aim at transcending camouflage. However, forms of camouflage are still employed at the social level as instrumental deception. Camouflaged behaviour in service of self-preservation, predation, and expression of aggression can be observed as highly homologous in function in all living species.

Eibl-Eibesfeldt (1989) has identified forms of phylogenetic regression in the area of sexual behaviour. He has described certain pathologies such as sexual sadism, and promiscuity as phylogenetic regressions to the archaic "reptilian stage" of agonistic sexuality. A similar regression in the area of the expression of aggression is hypothesized in the present book. The evolution of formal organizations has created an environment that discourages individuals from attacking or even confronting one another. Humans have adapted to the inhibition of aggression by the activation of archaic techniques of camouflage—techniques employed in almost every living species, from the simplest to most complex forms.

Society has "evolved" to the point where, in the expression of aggression, we have regressed to forms of behaviour that mirror the adaptation of insects, birds, and other animals which express aggression without detection.

Ethical Regression

Organizational complexity has not only engendered a regression to more primitive forms of aggression expression, it has also led to a regression in ethics and values.

Many social analysts have drawn attention to the constriction of ethical principles in the operation of organizations. Attempts at explaining this problem have almost invariably attributed the phenomenon to the nature of bureaucratic relationships. An example is Jackall's (1987) penetrating analysis of the difficulty of realizing personal ethical standards within the profit-based corporation. The gist of his analysis is that the bureaucracy tends to transform all moral issues into practical concerns. This is achieved through the organizational process which gradually redefines or operationalizes individual concerns and aspirations in terms of the corporate context. A major aspect of this process is a commitment to the norms of "pragmatic flexibility," norms which promote adaptiveness to inconsistency and to dexterity in meeting the conflicting expectations of diverse audiences. Pragmatism can supplant the abstract principles found in altruism, liberalism, humanism, and most of the other "isms" in modern society.

The basic practical principles of operation in corporate life according to Jackall (1988) can be stated briefly as:

(1) You never go around your boss. (2) You tell your boss what he wants to hear, even when your boss claims that he wants dissenting views. (3) If your boss wants something dropped, you drop it. (4) You are sensitive to your boss's wishes so that you anticipate what he wants; you don't force him, in other words, to act as boss. (5) Your job is not to report something that your boss

does not want reported, but rather to cover it up. You do what
your job requires, and you keep your mouth shut. (pp.109-10)

The abstract notions of allegiance and authority are operational-
ized in terms of personal relationships. When managers describe their
work to an outsider, they first say, "I work for Bill Jones" or "I report
to Harry Smith" before they proceed to describe their official functions. According to Jackall, success and failure within the corporation
become contingent upon cultivated political connections that foster
advancement and protect against sudden administrative shakeups or
irrational market changes. Accountability becomes contingent on political connections or on being in the right or wrong place rather than on
stable criteria. The anxiety generated by a sense of uncertainty and lack
of control over events creates a pressure toward team alliances. "Team
playing" requires "self-streamlining," where one makes oneself into an
object tailored to suit the context or the occasion. This uncertainty leads
to anxiety that one's job is always on the line and engenders a need to
protect oneself and, if possible, those within one's circle. When things
go wrong, the immediate reaction is to cya ("cover your ass"). When an
internal problem reaches public attention, and thereby poses a threat to
business operations, it is turned over to public relations, a place where
moral issues are managed as strategic tasks. Jackall ends his analysis
with the following conclusion:

A moral judgment based on a professional ethos has no meaning
in a world where the etiquette of authority relationships, non-
accountability for actions, and the necessity for protecting and
covering for one's boss, one's network, and oneself supersede
all other considerations. As a matter of survival, not to mention
advancement, corporate managers keep their eyes fixed on the
social framework of their world and its requirements. Thus,
they simply do not see most issues that confront them as moral
concerns, even when problems might be posed by others in moral
terms. (p. 105)

Jackall explains the neutralization of individual and professional ethics in organizations in terms of bureaucratically structured conditions and relationships. He argues that the uncertainty and anxiety experienced by employees working in profit-based corporations come to assume a pivotal position at the expense of other motivations. Jackall does not distinguish between profit and non-profit organizations and appears to confine his analysis to business corporations. However, a similar erosion of ethicality often takes place in stable non-profit organizations that do not subject employees to "survival" anxiety and intra-organization competitiveness, which calls into question the adequacy of an explanation that attributes the ethical decline solely to uncertainty and competitiveness.

Jackall's analysis assumes that the loss of ethicality is caused by the organizational structure and the relationships it creates. However, this book maintains that another force is at play: the phylogenetic regressive movement away from confrontation and toward camouflage. Thus, the structurally based suppression of confrontation within the organization has united (and catalysed) biological, psychological, and social forces to promote an ethic of fear, deception, subterfuge, and manipulation in the pursuit of organizational goals. I have observed three types of regression:

1. *Regression to egocentrism.* According to Kohlberg (1969), progress in moral reasoning involves a six-stage movement, from an egocentric view of what is good to one that is more abstract and universal. The operationalization of the individual's principles in terms of the organizational procedures and corporate objectives engenders forms of moral thinking that are concrete and curtailed in scope. The preoccupation with individual survival shifts the focus of moral concerns to what benefits the immediate network, department, or self at the expense of the welfare of clients and society. The norms of pragmatic flexibility further diffuse principled and categorical thinking. Both the concrete and the

self-centred perspectives represent a regression to the early stages of moral development employed in childhood.

2. *Regression from self as subject to self as object.* The perception of self as fundamentally contingent on organizational changes or on authority decisions is inherently limiting. Formal authority reinforces the social perception that the employee also represents an "honourable" or "decent" or "law-abiding" citizen. The individual in the diminished psychological state experiences the self as an object, something that gets "nailed" like a piece of wood or that gets on or off the "hook" like a fish. The experiencing of self as an object also promotes the adoption of Darwinian survivalist strategies, which tends to impede ethical and intellectual reflection. The perception and experience of self as a subject that is capable of holding and implementing value positions is necessary for the maintenance of ethical behaviour.

This regression to self as an object can be illustrated by the kinds of restrictions that employees experience in organizational settings. Many of these restrictions are actually self-imposed and are not requested by upper management. I have been, to my dismay, an observer of this kind of behaviour among senior researchers hired by a division of a federal ministry dealing with crime and rehabilitation. Some of these researchers sought to narrowly define their consultancy duties as purveyors of information and customized studies geared to meet upper management's didactic goals, and they further sought to intimidate colleagues who wanted to adhere to their more independent academic role, that of system analysis and of exploration of new approaches. Often such restriction of duties to passive pragmatics is neither a formal nor a functional organizational demand. During a meeting attended by the deputy minister, I asked him whether the ministry was only interested in operations advice; he replied that, to the contrary, the ministry welcomed new theoretical models and perspectives. Anti-intellectualism or intellectual curtailment may be catalysed by the regression of the self to the state of an object.

3. *Regression at the level of security.* In some cases, conditions can lead to a fear of retaliation, which can sometimes be unrealistic and exaggerated. Anxious, vulnerable individuals may be afraid to express their views directly or to take moral stands. This self-constricting fear that afflicts the bureaucrat is an intriguing phenomenon that can be explained in terms of phylogenetic regression. It is interesting to consider the symbolism of some of the vocabulary of bureaucracy which refer to the state of camouflage and a concern about its removal. This preoccupation indicates that camouflage is an underlying psychological reality within the organization: "pointing the finger at" (visual blowing of cover), "blowing the whistle" (auditory blowing of cover), "covering one's ass" (seeking cover after losing cover), "sticking one's neck out" (risking the loss of cover).

The need to maintain a state of camouflage can also be inferred from the trend to shy away from personal accountability. Jackall (1987), for example, describes how senior managers go to great lengths to avoid or minimize the effectiveness of inquiries seeking to identify personal accountability and use creative ploys to avoid being identified as perpetrator. For example, a high-ranking executive told Jackall, "The one statement that will paralyze a room is when someone in authority says: 'Now I'm not interested in a witch hunt, but...' When these words are uttered, the first reaction of people is immediately to hunker down and protect their flanks" (p. 100).

The reaction of many managers to novel and creative ideas is fear and anxiety related to self-preservation. In some instances, their fear is unrealistic, but the maxim "better safe than sorry" has become the *sine qua non* in the management of public organizations. How is it that accomplished individuals who occupy secure positions are so easily and irrationally intimidated by rather nebulous threats? What has happened to official status, to intellectual credibility, to the security of seniority and tenure, to pride of office, and even to vanity? Managers appear to have found it necessary to run into hiding, just as tiny birds hide and freeze when they see the shadow of a circulating hawk. The problem is not only that they hide in fear but also that after the perceived threat is gone, they are compelled to bolster their self-esteem. Often the individual who suggested the creative idea, or someone who is more vulnerable, is subjected to intimidation. The managers' actions are likely to be covered by a veneer of politically correct and organizationally supportive rhetoric which suppresses criticism. For these managers, feelings of powerlessness are assuaged by challenging the power of others. Managers can bring themselves up by knocking others down, as long as they are not seen to be doing so.

The Convergence on Injustice as a Form of Ethical Decline

The moral regression that takes place in organizations can be seen to affect ethical behaviour in two general ways: 1) the cultivation of moral callousness, and 2) the segmentation of the moral perspective. In both cases the causes are shown to inhere in the previously described processes of operationalization and competition, insecurity, and in the self-constriction resulting from a regression to the state of camouflage. Moral callousness is often seen in a lack of compassion or the reluctance to "stick one's neck out" in support of colleagues who get treated unjustly, despite the grave consequences for the victim. Moral segmentation occurs when one isolates the norms that pertain to the work environment from the values that govern one's family and other aspects of one's life. For example, a manager may casually partake in a decision that results in a devastating blow to the career and family of an employee but react with exaggerated guilt and self-recrimination upon forgetting to feed the neighbour's cat or failing to show for a social date.

To illustrate, the excessive retaliatory reaction of a director against a subordinate or a client is a familiar occurrence. The reaction may be due to a blow to the ego or to past interaction between the two or to personal idiosyncrasy. The influence of other interacting colleagues usually serves to tame the excessive reaction and leads to a fair resolution of the conflict. But the sobering and balancing influence of rational and ethical colleagues may not be found in many organizations. Instead, some may not only tolerate the unethical behaviour, but may further join forces to implement it. Regardless of the motive, whether it for gaining privileges or for appeasing the director, this type of collective behaviour represents another qualitative step in the direction of moral decline and regression.

The term "mobbing", which refers to aggression directed against an individual by a group, has been recently used to describe a type of collaborative behaviour, one that is increasingly seen in the workplace (Leymann, 1996; Duffy & Sperry, 2014). This behaviour also has a phylogenetic base. Ethologists such as Konrad Lorenz (1966) describe how a grazing herd or birds in flock formations can collectively attack (mob) and expel a single predator. A flock of swans, relying on strength in numbers, can swarm a fox and prevent it from targetting one of the swans as its prey. Mobbing can be expressed in any context, such as family, school, neighbourhood, community, and online. It is delivered by a variety of techniques and avenues such as rumour, intimidation, discreditation, creating confusion, and isolation. In the workplace, coworkers, superiors, or subordinates often "gang up" against an employee to force him or her out of the workplace. Types of mobbing behaviour and the phases that victims pass through have been thoroughly described by a number of authors, including Leymann, Duffy and Sperry.

In Islamic jurisprudence, the toleration or collaboration with an unjust conduct perpetrated by a group of interacting individuals (*igtemaa ala albatil*) is seen as a far more serious transgression than an offence committed by an individual alone. The group collaboration with unjust conduct actually involves two moral transgressions: 1) the carrying out of an offence against an individual, and 2) failure to live up to the religious-moral duty to instruct and dissuade the group against participating in the immoral conduct (*alnahi an almunkar*).

Thus, collective condoning of and participating (meeting, converging: *igtemaa*) in a wrongful act is a more serious transgression than that carried out by an individual alone because it also involves the failure to defend a challenge to a religious duty and the social value it protects. Alkarni (2017) noted in this context that this "convergence on injustice" is not a conspiracy to commit an unethical act. A conspiracy involves consensus and planning to commit an act, as in the case of a group of thieves plotting to rob a store, and as such, the conspiracy is a part of the crime. In the "convergence on injustice" there is usually no consensus, as the perpetrators do not engage in deliberate discussion or planning related to the offence; individuals may slip into it by default or through thoughtlessness. Convergence on injustice can also be seen as a failure in confrontation. The individuals failed: a) to bring the matter into full consciousness, and b) to morally mobilize the group against it.

Increasingly we are witnessing cases where the prejudiced decision of a director in an organizational setting develops into a symphony of willing implementers. Such collective behaviour in public service agencies, universities, and other leading institutions indicates a widespread deterioration in ethical conduct.

Incivility as Ethical Decline

Mores, manners, and etiquettes regulate social interaction. They prescribe forms of recommended behaviour (civility) within a social context; they make social interaction consistent and predictable, and protect the self from the encroachments of interacting others. Thus, norms of civility protect the physical, psychological, and social boundaries of the individual self. One important boundary is that of dignity, which upholds the social essence of the individual as an autonomous and worthy entity within society. Attacks on this sense of dignity or self-worth (honour) are usually met with strong reactions. Lack of civility, with its resultant encroachments on the boundaries of the self, lead to demoralization and aggression. Workplaces that show a lack of civility (e.g., rudeness, disrespect, yelling, swearing), show evidence of increased conflicts.

Faculty and student incivility in universities has been one of the subjects of academic research (e.g., Twale & De Luca, 2008; Knepp, 2012). Academic incivility is often reciprocal; both students and faculty may contribute to a climate of disrespect. Incivility in the classroom takes the form of harassment, disruptive behaviour, and many forms of camouflaged aggression, all of which are detrimental to the learning process.

Machiavellian Management and Ethical Decline

The main concern of this text is with the dynamics of camouflaged aggression, regardless of motivational factors that influence the perception or labelling of the behaviour. Just as the need for money does not explain why people steal (they also work to obtain money), motives related to financial gain, advancement, status, or retaliation do not necessarily explain why individuals resort to camouflaged aggression. This aggression requires more than motive; it needs formal instruments, organizational opportunity, and particular environmental pressures, as well as the lack of normative and legal controls, to flourish; in other words, it needs purpose and process.

There is, however, one overarching motive that encompasses every available tactic and often leads to obsessive preoccupation: the quest for power. This motive needs to be addressed briefly in relation to camouflaged aggression. "The acquisition of power is second only to money as a motivator for managers, executives, administrators, and professionals in a variety of occupations" (Sankar, 1994, p. 23). Power provides the leader with many practical and psychological rewards. Managers acquire their initial power base from the legitimate authority of their position. The quest for power tends to expand and intensify with new power gains. Successful managers are expected to have a greater need for power (in terms of contacts, influence, charisma) in order to perform effectively. But if this quest for power is not curtailed by the organization or by the personality of the individual, or by both, it will lead to the erosion of other important qualities of effective management and to the dysfunctional resort to camouflaged aggression.

Velasquez (1982) observed that managers use a variety of tactics to develop their power base, including image building, associating with influential individuals, forming alliances, employing trade-offs, controlling access to information, manipulating research data, making strategic replacements, creating sponsor-protegé relationships, neutralizing potential opposition, stimulating competition among ambitious subordinates, and restricting communication about real intentions. The realization of such objectives involves a heavy reliance on the camouflage of intentions and of actual goals.

Books that purport to teach tactics for organizational power can be seductive to many managers, particularly in settings affected by global competition and corporate takeovers, and within cultural institutions promoting individualism and self-aggrandizement. Examples of such books are G.R. Griffin's *Machiavelli on Management: Playing and Winning the Corporate Power Game* (1991, pp. x–xi), which seeks to "offer a concise guide to the principles of management as filtered through Machiavellian thought," and G.W. Fairholm's *Organizational Power Politics: Tactics in Organizational Leadership* (1993), which offers twenty-two power tactics for managers. The Machiavellian philosophy that underlies these approaches assumes that no good can be achieved without power, that power cannot be achieved without manipulation and deceit, and that manipulation is therefore necessary for the achievement of good. Effective manipulation presupposes an ability to camouflage intentions and goals through the deployment of techniques of false pretence and trickery.

Although Machiavellian power tactics can promote effective management, they engender two serious problems which the authors failed to address. First, the manager's successful pursuit of power games can become obsessive, addictive, and self-serving, as he or she progresses through the stages described below. Second, power games tend to be readily recognized, learned, and reciprocated in kind and to the extent that everyone in the organization comes to act like Machiavelli's prince. Stringent organizational controls against the indulgence in power games is necessary.

A progressive deterioration in the style of the manager who resorts to Machiavellian power tactics can develop along three stages:

1. *Benign stage*. Using power tactics without intention to deceive or harm others.
2. *Manipulation stage*. Active and conscious manipulation of the truth and deliberate deception.
3. *Autonomy stage*. Incorporation of manipulation and deception as the managerial strategies of choice. Camouflaged aggression is no longer simply a means to an end; it is an end in itself.

Even one pathological manager who has reached Stage 3 can have an enormously destructive effect on an organization and its members. Camouflaged aggression seems to have an infectious quality. When many managers and members come to function at Stage 3, the organization itself can be said to have reached Stage 3. At that stage it is pathological and will soon become dysfunctional. It got that way by its failure to prevent the rampant use of camouflaged tactics such as bluffing, conning, gamesmanship, and intimidation, and by failing to maintain values which would make such activities unacceptable.

PATTERNS OF CAMOUFLAGED AGGRESSION

THERE ARE PROBABLY AS MANY TECHNIQUES for camouflaging aggression as there are people who apply them. Systems of advanced technology are continuously creating new avenues for the delivery of aggression, ones that may be variants of the traditional forms we are most familiar with. These traditional forms can be classified according to the following categories.

1. Indecision

Many bureaucrats display a chronic tendency toward decision avoidance and ambivalence. This indecision, which may represent a level of psychological insecurity, may, at the same time, be employed as a technique of camouflaged aggression. Such individuals often delay making any decision or taking any action until all the (often unnecessary) information has been obtained or until all the (often disinterested) authorities have been consulted, or until the decision has been turned over to a committee. It is ironic that individuals who have a secure position, seniority, credibility, education, and experience often avoid taking a position on issues, or eagerly comply with the expectations of higher authority and accommodate their views even if they do not agree with them. An exaggerated, almost paranoid, fear appears to grip the will of many bureaucrats. Their trepidation, which hinders open and direct expression of feelings, may earn them contempt. Their behaviour is akin to the freezing behaviour exhibited by many animals and may represent a regression along the phylogenetic continuum of camouflage. Many animals freeze behind camouflage in the presence of a potential attacker in order to minimize detection. A human form of freezing is indecision.

In organizations, the self-protective strategy of freezing can also be accompanied by the second strategy of camouflage: the efficient delivery of aggression. Indecision can thus be employed as a technique for hurting others through frustration and exasperation.

2. Rigidity

Indecision can hurt, so can rigidity. Bureaucrats can readily express aggression by refusing to allow or accommodate change. Change can be an anathema to a bureaucrat not only because it involves risk but also because it implies that what the bureaucrat is currently doing is somehow flawed. Bureaucrats are often threatened by creativity. It makes them uncomfortable. Many make a show of publicly encouraging creativity and applauding new ideas while they retaliate against creative thinkers.

Bureaucrats can easily make a simple idea or initiative complex, so complex that it requires careful study (referral to a committee) or more information (referral to consultants) or careful costing (referral to accountants). As a last resort, it can be referred to lawyers. Each of these apparently sensible precautions can effectively kill a proposal. They may not be precautions but merely ploys. They can be time-consuming and expensive and are likely to require extra work from other members of the organization, who, in turn, may come to resent the initiator.

3. Time Manipulation

Time can hurt. Time can be an effective weapon. Those who wish to inflict suffering have two choices: they can rush you or delay you, and they can do both while appearing to act in your best interest.

Too Little Time

Most of us recognize the discomfort that someone can make us feel with a glance at their watch while we are talking to them. It is a simple gesture but one which can ruin your concentration in a conversation or ruin your presentation at a meeting. Nothing need be said; no ill feelings need be expressed. In fact, the more surreptitious the glance, the more the speaker is hurt. A direct communication from the listener that he has little time would be less discomforting than a more furtive glance at a watch.

Most of us have experienced the ill feeling created by a bureaucrat who shuns us by perennially telling us "sorry I'm in a meeting at the moment," or by entering a euphemistic message on the answering machine about not being available. This serves to communicate, without seeming to do so, that we are unimportant.

Most of us have had the experience of arriving at a meeting with bureaucrats who, apologizing profusely, inform us that they soon have to attend a meeting which they just learned about; they thereby lower our self-esteem as we realize that we are less important in their eyes than the people they are about to meet with, whoever they may be. As Ross (1999) has noted, meetings become more important than people.

Too Much Time

A much more common technique is to take too much time. It is easy to make you suffer by creating a delay which is "in your best interest" or in the service of "procedure" or "policy" or "doing it right."

Formality can be a polite, even graceful, way to ensure you suffer by delay. Phrases such as "we will just get the paperwork done first"; "I am sure he will wish to give it his personal attention"; "we really should check with..."; and "it is being processed" are all familiar ways to keep you waiting and wondering. They also take your control away.

Even more irritating are delays which you must endure because of "policy." "Policy" is most likely to be invoked when your attempt to complain makes the person who is delaying you resentful of your challenging them, their position, or their authority. It is understood that you must not be aggressive toward the person who is delaying you; after all they are only following policy and are not personally responsible for your distress (although you may suspect they are delighting in the opportunity to use their position and "policy" to make you suffer). Bureaucrats are safely protected by "established procedure." They can use their positions to inflict wounds while making any objection against them appear to be inappropriate, unfair, and socially unacceptable.

You can, of course, question the policy or express your disdain for it and suggest that you or the bureaucrat should take action to have it changed. Such presumptuous behaviour is likely to lead to your being pictured in the eyes of the bureaucrat, observing bystanders, and eventually yourself as an imbecile for even *thinking* that policy can be challenged, let alone changed.

Typically, the delay is accompanied by an explanation that one's choices are limited. The implication is that because the bureaucrat's freedom of choice and power have been taken away by the organization, yours must be too. Bureaucrats reduce you to their level of impotence while they exercise the only power the organization has left them—the power to make you suffer. They are protected by organizational procedures which are "designed to protect you" but actually have you at their mercy.

It should be noted in this context that the suffering inflicted as a result of delay does not stem only from the frustration in need fulfilment. It is also augmented by a universal existential condition, in that an individual's lifespan is finite. For example, the delay in the payment of an invoice may block a long-planned and much-needed vacation. The suffering stems, not only from the blockage of a desire, but also from an implicit awareness that there may not be many other convenient times for such a vacation: life does not go on forever. Thus, delays chip away at our finite duration (our life); they constitute, in the final analysis, attempts at slow killing. Delays can result from "red tape"; they also can be precipitated by an administrator who wields the "hand that kills tenderly," to borrow a phrase of Nietzsche's (1886/1967, p. 42), one who can only relate to a passive and whimpering experience of destruction and death. The challenge in dealing with this form of camouflaged aggression is to distinguish between delay stemming from structural sources and delay stemming from human intention masked by the former.

4. Waiting as a Status Degradation Ceremony

To be kept waiting unduly to meet an official is another way time can be used to deliver camouflaged aggression. Excessive waiting is likely to eat away at our self-esteem and self-confidence and to compromise our performance in a scheduled meeting. This prolonged waiting can also provoke anger. This anger may be neutralized by the apologetic rationalizations of the official and by the victim's fear of losing whatever he or she has at stake in the meeting. In some Arab countries, the anger of an individual waiting for an official is neutralized by hospitality in the form of offering coffee, juice, and expensive sweets. Thus, the victim's anger, but not resentment, can be safely neutralized. Resentment at the assault on self-esteem, however, is likely to linger.

5. Information Manipulation

Knowledge is power, but it is through the controlled dissemination of information that power is exercised. The manipulative withholding and distribution of information is the basis of much camouflaged aggression:

Too Much Information

The person who coined the phrase "sticks and stones may break my bones but names will never hurt me" never worked in an organization. Many careers have been ruined by gossips. Rumour mongers are often trivialized as individuals who enliven their lacklustre personal lives by gossiping. I suggest their gossiping can also be an expression of hostility as well as boredom. Many are individuals who would never dare to express something critical to anyone directly but relish in criticizing individuals behind their backs. Such backstabbing is an everyday occurrence in organizations which strive to present an image of polite interaction among their members. Simple gossip is an obvious weapon of the aggressor. Much more devious and camouflaged are techniques involving innuendo, innocent-appearing rumour dropping, "accidental" breaches of confidential information; question-raising ("do you *really* think *she* could do *that?*"), and feigned denial ("I don't believe *she* would do that"). Fabrication is less likely to be used than exaggeration of an actual event.

Destructive information dissemination need not be nasty. You can quickly and effectively be driven up the wall by someone who helps you too much by giving you more information than you could possibly want or comprehend. All of us can be driven to distraction by the pedantic individual who tries too hard to help us by giving us too much detail or too much advice. In fact, a common form of bureaucratic sabotage consists of subordinates deliberately providing or subjecting their supervisors to "information overload" in order to drive them into a state of confusion and self-doubt.

Too Little Information

Just as destructive as disseminating information is withholding or delaying the release of useful information. We can be subjected to agonizing doubt and worry by an apparently well-meaning individual who withholds or delays giving us information because "I didn't want to hurt your feelings" or "I didn't know how to tell you," or "I delayed saying anything until I was really sure."

Another form of indirect aggression involves softening the blow by giving you only that amount of information which is not likely to upset you or by euphemizing the information that is given to you so that you do not seek more. In both cases the information is withheld under the guise of helping you or easing your pain. The implication is that your pain would have been magnified if you had been given all the information; the reality is that withholding the information was intended to avoid your anger. Minimizing or restricting information is sometimes designed to enable harmful acts to be perpetrated in such a way as to minimize the risk of retaliation (e.g., by lawsuit) by the person who has been injured.

The Building of Information

It has become very difficult to terminate employment or other forms of membership in an organization. One has to "build up a file" over a period of months or years to justify the ultimate punishment. Whereas one can appreciate the justice of basing termination on such documentation, it takes little imagination to realize the enormously destructive power the surveillance and detailed recording of our behaviour involve. We now are fired in stages, which means that our suffering is prolonged. Such procedures may improve objectivity but they also engender suspiciousness, fear, insecurity, and animosity among employers and employees. Gone are the days when disgruntled employers or employees would confront each other about some incident at the time it happened. Now they hold their ill feelings in check until the annual performance review, which may be months down the road. Supervisors behave politely and courteously, and express concern for one another's welfare, as they make careful notes on a file which, when the time comes, will be used to justify terminating the employee in an apparently objective manner, devoid of any display of personal animosity or vindictiveness. Camouflaged aggression is often dispensed slowly and carefully.

The Timing of Information

The choice of time in releasing information is a central factor in maximizing its harmful impact. It is not *that* the information is being released but also *when* it is released that determines the harm. For example, the delivery of a termination notice (usually by email—the current equivalent of the infamous "pink slip") is usually strategically timed to reach its victim late Friday afternoon or at the beginning of a holiday. The news not only ruins his or her weekend or vacation, it also makes him or her suffer the torments of being deprived of avenues for immediate redress. Also, managers do not want to get you while you are hot.

6. Control by Overwork

As discussed above, camouflaged aggression can be delivered through the manipulation of time and timing. Here the subjective time of the employee and his or her energy is constricted through extensive work demands. When a senior employee is overwhelmed by work demands, he or she is less likely to engage in critical challenges, political ambitions, or innovative behaviour that may interfere with the agendas of superiors. Many senior employees, in both the private and public sectors, are compelled to take work home to fulfil the heavy demands of their various responsibilities. To ensure compliance with such stressful demands for lengthy periods of time, two conditions are necessary: 1) the employee must be working on a project or on tasks that are highly relevant to his or her expertise, professional interests, and promotion, and 2) the employee must be well paid. Thus, overwhelming the attention of an employee is a way of exerting control; this can be achieved by imposing a heavy workload that is highly compensated.

7. Withdrawal

The withdrawal of love is frequently used in families to express displeasure when a family member does something offensive. This process has its parallel in organizations. In organizations, it is not love which is withheld, it is attention. People can lower your self-esteem more effectively by ignoring you than by rebuking you. If your colleague sharply rebukes you, it may hurt, but at least you know they are angry with you and probably why. However, their ignoring you may mean that many things about you are displeasing them, things you are left to conjecture and feel guilty about.

In organizations, the withdrawal of attention is frequently done not directly (e.g., "I am angry and don't want to speak to you"), but indirectly (e.g., "I am sorry I am not available to answer the phone at the moment") through voicemail.

A strategy often deployed for control by means of withdrawal takes place when a new employee is awarded affection, concern, and support, but is treated with coolness and rejection soon after settling into the new position. In other words, "affective capital" invested in that individual is withdrawn. This practice can be used by coworkers as well as by supervisors, and results in anxiety, distress, and diminished confidence in the targetted individual, who is left in a state of vulnerability to manipulation and compliance.

Much more destructive than temporary withdrawal of attention or support is *intermittent* withdrawal which leaves you wondering not only *why* you are being rejected but *when* you will be rejected again. The manager who alternates between bursts of affectionate recognition and unexpected withdrawal creates a generalized state of apprehension and psychological vulnerability. Such practices can become so well entrenched within the corporate culture that they are expressed spontaneously and unconsciously.

A related construct that involves withdrawal practices is ostracism, where the ignoring, the exclusion, and the overlooking are typically orchestrated by a group. Ostracism becomes an ambiguous experience as it involves the absence rather than the presence of a behaviour. Defining it becomes difficult owing to the difficulty of assessing intentionality. Robinson and Schabram (2017) analyze this construct and recommend further research on this underexamined type of workplace aggression.

8. Inaccessibility

Any administrator, regardless of rank, can make access to him- or herself a difficult, frustrating, and time-consuming exercise. A vast and expanding range of measures, techniques, and devices are available in any organization that can keep one in abeyance and in a state of anxiety. They include the use of an intermediary, such as a secretary who politely informs you that the boss is in a meeting (whether or not that is the case), and the now ever-present voicemail, which gives us no choice but to talk only to a machine. All can be employed to erect a temporal and spatial barrier, one that can be used selectively. Not only does the elusive administrator avoid confrontation with a problem you may wish to present, he or she also has the opportunity to express camouflaged aggression. Blocking our efforts to resolve a pressing issue not only increases our frustration, but, at the same time, prevents us from expressing our aggression against its source. Deprived of a target, we are likely to direct our anger elsewhere or to turn it inward, against ourselves. Either way, the administrator can sit back comfortably and enjoy the fruits of his or her efforts to distress us without having to face us.

Consider the negative social implications of a relatively new invention, namely, voicemail, a system which structures its own forms of trickery. To be able to find out who has called you while you were out of the office is a significant and a low-cost service. However, relying on voicemail in the daily operations of offices of public institutions or large corporations can have serious detrimental effects on clients. This device can readily be used as an effective aid to preventing accessibility. The personal voicemail of the employee delivers to the client an instant temporal block that is both frustrating and demoralizing, particularly when the message states that the incumbent is in his or her office but away from his or her desk. This technology maximizes the rewards of inaccessibility in favour of the employee within the organization. The employee can sit back and judge (often on the basis of a limited or fragmented message) when, or whether, to return the call, knowing that any decision he or she makes can be justified in ways that the client has no means of verifying.

Thus, devices and procedures that promote inaccessibility represent an assault on the confrontational strategy itself. For example, an occupant of a public office, such as a professor, may not keep regular office hours or a secretary to book appointments; appointments are booked through his or her voicemail, which often goes unanswered. Such inaccessibility allows the incumbent to relinquish duties, and feeds his or her narcissism in having people strive for his or her valuable attention.

Inaccessibility structures such as those described above have been giving rise to new forms of organizational behaviour. When lower and junior managers become inaccessible, clients sometimes resort to receptions and private parties so that they can directly or personally meet with these junior managers. Thus, inaccessibility can engender a *flattening* of lobbying.

9. Non-interference

One of the subtle ways of delivering aggression occurs when supervisors or coworkers choose not to interfere, correct, or warn another employee who is making a mistake or who is unwittingly indulging in a behaviour that is likely to get him or her into trouble. The aggressors may justify their inaction to themselves and others by voicing their concern that interference would involve a violation of values such as respect for privacy and individual freedom of choice. Non-interference is often a way of venting aggression, one which allows the aggressor to sit back and enjoy watching individuals harm themselves.

10. Entrapment

Entrapment in the animal world involves an aggressor acting in some beguiling way which leads its prey into suspending its self-protective behaviour, or by leading it to enter a place where it can be devoured. The Venus flytrap, for example, displays a fake flower to attract insects, whereupon it traps them for a meal. Entrapment in the organizational environment usually involves luring one's victim by warmth and understanding into making mistakes. For example, potential victims can be seduced into expressing genuine feelings or revealing information which can be used against them in other situations. Entrapment relies on the skills of masking genuine feelings and intentions through false representation.

I had one experience with entrapment which I cannot resist sharing, one in which I was the victim. I had submitted a brief proposal for a training program to a director in a public agency, who, as I found out later, was developing a similar program of his own. During our meeting, in which another member of his department was present, he proceeded to discuss the practical administrative implications of my program on the assumption that it had been accepted. This "assumption" was skilfully conveyed, in the course of the discussion, to give the impression of a tacit acceptance of my program, which thus encouraged me to hand to the director large parts of its contents. The director was able to put his hands on the material by entrapping me with deferential flattery and by giving the false impression that I had been hired.

11. Random Kindness

A manager may impetuously lavish extensive help on an unsuspecting client or employee who neither asked for nor expected such concern. This random and extravagant kindness often takes the form of giving information and advice with affected politeness and sympathy. There may be at least four reasons for the manager's sudden burst of goodness: 1) atonement for rudeness or unfair treatment of another employee or client, 2) self-aggrandizement in front of staff, 3) neutralization of the impact of negative deeds perpetrated elsewhere, and 4) spite for an enemy or victim who was exposed to his nasty side, implying "I was nasty to you because you deserved it; but, after all, I am a nice person."

12. Subordination via Sexualization

Physical attractiveness is valued in members of both sexes, arguably more so for women than for men. The combination of formal authority and sexual signals, whether intended or not, creates a power-related dynamic in the workplace. The social exchange theory (Homans, 1961) provides some insight into this dynamic. It defines power as a differential between possession of valued assets and the need of others for these assets. For example, if a person has control over certain resources and is reluctant or under no obligation to give them to another person who wants them, the first party automatically assumes a level of power over the second. The attraction of one person to the exposed or suggested sexual assets of another, and their restriction by virtue of formal distance, can put the former in a submissive or compromised position of power in relation to the latter and to their formal authority. This subordination can take the form of curtailing critical attitudes toward the coveted individuals or accommodating their interests or wishes. Any residue of guilt from the initial attraction will compound the psychological subordination. This power dynamic can apply to both men and women as they occupy positions as managers or employees. Although many women and men look down at and resist engaging in this sexualized communication, still many may resort to it consciously or spontaneously. With the consolidation of the gender shift in high managerial positions, sexual charisma may become routinized similar to the routinization of political charisma after the consolidation of a new order, as described by Max Weber (1947). Routinization of sexual charisma need not result in the extinction of the power dynamics.

13. Undermining the Sense of Security

A variety of strategies can be deployed to undermine the sense of security of an employee. A common strategy is the dissemination of indirect, incomplete, or negative information regarding impending cuts or terminations, or with respect to the performance of an employee. The resulting anxiety and distress not only handicap the performance of the victim, but also render him or her vulnerable to manipulation, exploitation, and domination.

Large numbers of employees can be made to comply with adverse policies and conditions through the anxiety provoked by the threat of budget cuts, layoffs, downsizing, and the like. One of the main dangers of provoking this type of existential anxiety lies in its undermining of employee morale and creative initiative, as these are contingent upon a sense of security and acceptance cultivated by the corporate body. Crafty managers who employ these tactics are aware of their limitations. Excessive insecurity may too easily be perceived as a threat and can lead to open hostility or sabotage. However, an intermittent provocation of anxiety can enhance subordination and compliance. Tacit threats need to be followed, after a time, by reprieves, such as the suspension of the threat or offer of some future reward. Regardless of functional benefits to the organization, such as compliance, these security-undermining tactics can exert a heavy toll in terms of increased resentment, apathy, and lowered productivity.

14. Ego Bashing

This form of camouflaged aggression typically targets the total self or ego of the victim rather than the extensions of the self. Reprimands directed at extensions of the self, such as an employee's decisions, management style, conduct, or productivity, are easier to handle. But attacks that target, symbolically and socially, a person's ego or sense of self-worth are difficult to endure or manage. For instance, the victim's telephone calls or emails may go unanswered; he or she may not be invited to a meeting that falls within his or her concern or is dropped from a guest list to a reception at the manager's house, or his or her presence is ignored during a meeting. Unlike the previously described techniques involving withdrawal, undermining the sense of security, and waiting, which focus on a certain aspect of vulnerability, the aggression in this case is directed at the victim's entire ego, status, and sense of self-worth. I have studied this behaviour in an Arabian Gulf country that is undergoing rapid social change (Abdennur, 2013). Two main causes of the behaviour are suggested: status inconsistency and narcissism. Status inconsistency arises in cases where an individual occupies a high position but lacks the needed technical or intellectual skills, where an individual is given high status but little power or a small salary, or where he or she comes from a prestigious family but occupies a low-prestige job. Such discrepancies can generate embarrassment and strain within the incumbent. The organizational position of the incumbent is also tied to the narcissism of the extended family, with its collective image and prestige. This narcissistic incorporation of extended family status compounds the threat of status inconsistency. Thus, status inconsistency can create a psychological strain in the employee who seeks to lower the strain by displacing his aggression on vulnerable others in the workplace. Since his or her total self-worth has been challenged, he or she will target the entire sense of self-worth or ego of other employees.

15. The Bureaucratic Vendetta

The urge to retaliate or reciprocate aggression in a camouflaged manner does not appear to be diminished by the passage of time and even at the level of petty grievances. Grudges for slights are not abandoned; they are held in a state of suspended animation until an organizational opportunity arises for retaliation. Furthermore, continuous, cordial, and direct interactions do not appear to eliminate the protagonists' need for getting even. This state of vengeful rumination contrasts with that of confrontative retaliation, where the direct catharsis and the conflict resolution that ensue often reduce the need to retaliate. But there may be more to bureaucratic vendetta than the blocking of direct catharsis.

I suggested in Chapters 1 and 2 that the confrontational and non-confrontational modes are qualitatively different and that the former is more advanced from an evolutionary perspective and healthier for social and individual well-being. Choosing to deliver aggression in a non-confrontational, rather than a confrontational, mode involves a crucial point of conversion at the psychological level. This point of conversion is a *modal shift* from a forthright and direct approach to one of deception and camouflage. The most important differences between these two strategies lie in the *affective* and *temporal* dimensions. Thus, an individual opting to aggress through the non-confrontational mode will have to suppress or repress the affective components, namely, anger, hostility, and opposition, and replace them with a retrograde and masked vindictiveness that publicly announces that "there is no problem." The shift from a strategy of attack to one of camouflage also implies opting for a protracted, time-oriented expression of aggression, usually involving surveillance and waiting for the right opportunity. The correspondence of this choice to phylogenetically rooted strategies is clear: most of what the camouflaged animal does is wait quietly and calmly for the right opportunity to strike. A preying cat may lie for hours in wait in front of a mouse hole. Thus, the regressed phylogenetic-psychological state combines with the organizational structure to make bureaucratic revenge a waiting and timing game.

The Hydraulic Principle

The ethologist Konrad Lorenz (1966) postulated that human aggression springs primarily from an innate fighting instinct, one that is necessary for species survival. He believed that aggression is not necessarily the result of a reaction to external stimuli; it can be spontaneously generated. He believed that energy specific to aggression accumulates continuously in the neural centres and that the accumulated energy seeks discharge regardless of the presence of a triggering stimulus. Although animals and humans both tend to respond to specific "releasers" of aggressive energy, humans do not just passively await the proper releasers, they spontaneously search for or invent them. "It is the spontaneity of the instinct that makes it so dangerous" (Lorenz, 1966, p. 76).

Freud (1917/1965) also argued that aggression, defined as physical and psychological destructiveness expressed against others and/or the self, is not merely a reaction to external stimuli nor is it restricted to ego preservation; it is a constantly flowing impulse rooted in the constitution of the human organism: in effect, a death instinct. In his final conceptualization, aggression is rooted in the tendency toward biological disintegration or death and is inescapable. His conception suggests that concern should be focused not on the elimination of aggression (for that is impossible), but on its deflection, management, and sublimation.

Conceptions of aggression such as those of Freud and Lorenz have been referred to as *hydraulic models* of aggression. The analogy refers to the pressure exercised by dammed-up water or steam in a closed container. The hydraulic model of aggression is based on two assumptions:

1. Aggression is generated from internal sources and from external stimuli and tends to accumulate until it is discharged.
2. The accumulated aggression, as in the case of dammed water, is expressed at the point of least resistance or the weakest or least defended point.

There is no intention at this point to argue about the first assumption; it has been debated for generations. The interest here is in the second assumption since it pertains to the dynamics of the expression of aggression. Henceforth, for the purposes of this book, the hydraulic expression of aggression refers to the tendency for aggression to be expressed in accordance with the principle of least resistance.

Ethologists (e.g., Goodall, 1965; Lorenz, 1966) have conducted numerous studies and experiments among animals that demonstrate how aggression can be redirected to the closest, most convenient, or "safest" target. For example, if a chimpanzee is attacked by one of higher rank, it often does not dare fight back, but vents its aggression on one of lower rank. During the mating season, the female goose is allowed to invade the territory of the male; the gander deals with the triggered aggression by attacking an inanimate object such as a stone. Although among humans, social conventions have conditioned the expression of aggression, the displacement of aggression has been well documented in clinical and experimental research (e.g., see Feshbach & Singer, 1957; Berkowitz, Cochran, & Embree, 1981; Tedeschi & Norman, 1985; Miller, Pedersen, Earleywine, & Pollock, 2003). In many circumstances, human aggression can elude social conditioning and follow a hydraulically displaced route in which it is released at targets that present points of least resistance. The result, as shall be shown, is often dehumanization and social regression.

The Hydraulics of Human Aggression

The expression of aggression following the hydraulic model is a common occurrence in organizations. In many instances, and contrary to basic norms of fairness, aggression follows the course of least resistance. For example, the apparent target of a manager's reprimand is often the meek employee who is unlikely to protest and challenge the manager during a meeting. A manager angered by a serious transgression by some of his or her employees may resort to venting aggression during a general meeting and by directing criticism at the group as a whole to avoid direct confrontation with the actual employees who were at fault. During prison riots, which are usually characterized by unrestrained aggression, prisoners who get beaten up as "informants" often belong to the ranks of weak or undefended inmates.

Masri (1984) analyzed cases of non-combatant, innocent civilians killed during the Lebanese Civil War (1975–1990) in acts of retaliation and revenge. The victims were apparently killed on the basis of their nominally belonging to an opposing religious sect or political party. However, closer analysis revealed that their affiliation was a sufficient reason for their murder only when they presented a target of zero resistance to the highly armed and highly charged fighters. Those enraged fighters seeking revenge ignored the culpable, but armed, militia members close by and chose to vent their murderous aggression on the unarmed civilians. The civilian victims were convenient targets who promised no retaliatory response.

The principle of least resistance has been recognized, if not articulated, more than five hundred years ago when Machiavelli warned his prince not to travel about his people without armed escort. He apparently believed that no matter how meagre the armed escort was, it was enough, at least symbolically, to move the prince out of the vulnerable state of representing zero resistance in the face of volatile aggression. Machiavelli may have been aware that the presence of a small, crude force can at times be a better harness to dammed aggression than any appeal to fairness or reason.

The hydraulic relationship can also be observed in folk wisdom. There is an old Arab saying: "The one who intervenes to separate two individuals engaged in a fight will receive two-thirds of the blows." From the perspective of the hydraulic model, the two fighting parties are fully charged and actively aggressive while the peacemaker is less charged and less belligerent; the peacemaker represents a weaker point than any of the two combatants. As a result, blows land spontaneously on him. Those experienced at stopping fights, such as police officers, are aware of this relationship and often begin their intervention with an authoritarian burst of verbal and physical force. This initial action not only distracts the combatants but communicates that the intervenor is not a safe target.

The Hydraulics of Camouflaged Aggression

The hydraulic model suggests that aggression continually seeks discharge. It also suggests that when discharge in the direction of the original trigger of the aggression is blocked, it is likely to be redirected to some safer target. Aggression expressed through organizational structures, as in the case of rage, also follows hydraulic expression. In effect, the hydraulic expression of aggression is maximized at both extreme ends: high affect (extreme rage) and low affect (camouflaged expression). This paradox can be explained by the fact that in both of these two conditions there is often an absent or a weakened confrontational retaliatory force. Another reason for the choice of hydraulic expression is the weakening of the operations of moral norms. In the case of extreme rage, ethical consciousness is displaced by the strong affect; in the case of camouflaged aggression, ethical consciousness is weakened by the masking (no external audience) and by the fragmentation of the perception of the aggressive behaviour.

The blockage of confrontational aggression can be the result of a lack of opportunity or of the aggressor's judgment that the possible consequences of direct expression of aggression would make it unwise. The rules and conventions of organizations make such blockage commonplace. Accordingly, one would expect that aggression would be redirected to safer targets. An example would be "backstabbing" directed at an absent employee by his or her coworkers during a meeting. The absence of the target creates a point of low resistance or low deterrence, which both motivates and gives latitude to the expression of aggression. Similarly, many journal articles and books being considered for publication get subjected to unfair and vicious evaluations by reviewers. Such destructive critiques are often facilitated by the cloak of anonymity afforded to reviewers.

Favourite targets are employees who are part-time, on contract, or on probation. Such individuals are vulnerable because they have less recourse to retaliation and have more to lose in doing so compared with permanent, unionized, and tenured employees. This state of low resistance within the organization tends to attract spontaneous "free-floating" aggression and may lead to the victimization of such incumbents.

If the victim were to directly pose the question, "Why are you making me suffer?" the perpetrator, if he or she were to answer truthfully, would say, "because I can." Let me offer an illustration. A doctor discreetly leaves a bottle of pain pills close to a terminal patient in a humanitarian gesture, one that would allow her to terminate her suffering. The patient takes the pills and dies. When an attending nurse discovers the pills, she erupts into an exaggerated expression of ethical concern, aimed at exposing the doctor. Her reaction may very likely have more to do with the hydraulic situation than medical ethics. Her scruples were aroused as a result of the emergence of an opportunity she could use to hurt the doctor.

The hydraulic expression of aggression tends to target the most vulnerable, but in many organizations, vulnerability is a function not only of the perceived weakness of the person but also of the perceived weakness of the *position* the person occupies. In effect, individuals tend to be victimized because they are situationally vulnerable. The implication of this phenomenon is very significant; it involves a dehumanization of aggression which is essentially regressive. The selection of victims is determined not by their personal contribution to the actions which stimulated the aggressive feelings, or even by their personal attributes. It is determined by the *attributes of their situation.*

It is worth noting in this context that the vulnerable position not only attracts free-floating aggression via displacement but also gradually elicits latent aggression. For example, a vulnerably positioned employee may gradually draw out jealousy, status rivalry, and need for ego aggrandizement from colleagues and subordinates. Conversely, an incumbent with a fortified position (e.g., clear job description, tenure, unionization, recourse to protective legislation) would force his coworkers to suppress or to sublimate those aggressive feelings.

Victimology is the branch of criminology that examines not only the effect of crime on victims but also the contribution of the victim to the crime. It may be necessary to talk about *victimology of positions.* The weak or vulnerable position can contribute to antisocial aggressive behaviour in at least four major ways: 1) it hydraulically attracts free-floating aggression; 2) it cultivates and elicits aggressive expressions among interacting others; 3) it fails to provide sufficient deterrence; and

4) it runs the risk of causing the incumbent to lash out with excessive aggression after repeated assaults on his or her status or dignity.

Regressive Aggression

It has been argued that the reliance on camouflage in the expression of aggression in social settings represents a reversal of the evolutionary trend toward confrontation. Social development enabled aggressive impulses to be expressed more openly, consciously, and normatively against selected targets.

The socially meaningful and potentially valuable expression of aggression is lost when it is reducible to mere emotional or physical release. Cognitive, social, moral, and political considerations and goals must be integral parts of the expression of aggression in social behaviour. When these *a priori* considerations are no longer relevant to the expression of aggression, the behaviour is regressive. As will be discussed further in Chapter 5, the occurrence of random killings reflect this phenomenon. The rise in such crimes symbolizes the movement toward the indiscriminate expression of aggression. In random murder the aggressive drive is independent of purposeful social action. Thus, "aggression which can be socially meaningful and instrumental behaviour becomes an alien and purposeless tension that needs to be reduced like tension in a full bladder" (Abdennur, 1987, p. 122).

Hydraulically expressed aggression within an organization is de-symbolized, ego-alien, asocial, and dehumanized, and is therefore regressive. This regressive form of aggression can be termed malignant as it possesses similar characteristics to those of malignancies in biological processes. The most distinguishing feature of a malignant cell is that it is dissociated and behaves independently of its original function in the larger biological context. The cancer cell, unlike healthy cells, behaves in a fashion which is self-serving and free of the constraints that apply to the other cells. Malignant aggression in organizations is also self-serving and is not connected to higher social and political purposes;

its expression is situationally determined and its purpose is the release of tension. Thus, it becomes possible to give a clear definition to the term "malignant aggression," often employed metaphorically in the context of brutality. Malignant aggression refers to *aggressive behaviour that is expressed independently of its normative, social, and political contexts, and is precipitated solely by the need for tension release and a convenient situation.*

Self-Destructiveness in Organizations

The blockage of the flow of aggression also leads to the displacement of aggression onto another safe target—the self. Self-destructiveness is expressed not only in terms of behaviours such as self-flagellation, self-mutilation, or suicide. Aggression against self is more likely to be delivered non-confrontationally, that is without the victims realizing they are making themselves suffer or realizing that their suffering is attributable to aggression (see Karl Menninger's *Man against Himself*, first published in 1938). Self-directed aggression can take many forms such as industrial "accidents" and "unintentional" lapses in behaviour or judgment. Many executives have jeopardized themselves by behaving in ways which would not have been expected of them, given their abilities and experience. Self-destructiveness may, for example, make use of the simple act of forgetting in order to deliver a sabotaging blow to oneself or one's career. One may forget a deadline, an inspection, an appointment with an employer, a policy directive, or a safety measure. In situations where organizational structures preclude delivery of both confrontational and non-confrontational aggression against others, self-destructiveness can be expected to escalate and become the aggression of choice.

Self-directed aggression conforms to the hydraulic model since the self is a relatively safe target and promises little retaliation. Self-directed aggression is not only organizationally masked, it requires no acknowledgment since the aggressor is the victim. Self-deception acting in defence of self-image further enhances the masking of aggression against the self.

Technological and organizational complexity also creates a new quantitative relationship that can further contribute to existential unhappiness. The many tasks for managing everyday living nowadays tend to increase risk for making mistakes, misapplications, and bad choices. The problematic aspect of this relationship is that our consciousness becomes more preoccupied with things that go wrong and need fixing than with things that go well. The negative feedback from things that go wrong during a day (problems with electronic devices, financial transactions, cars, insurance, time schedules) far exceeds the positive feedback. This growing imbalance in favour of negative feedback may be responsible for the increase in the incidence of mild depression.

In his book *Civilization and Its Discontents*, Freud (1930/1961) argued that civilization imposes restrictions and delays on the gratification of the sexual and the aggressive instincts, and as culture evolves, more sacrifices are demanded of these instincts. He also predicted that advancements in civilization will be accompanied by further intensification of individuals' sense of guilt. The sense of guilt arises from the suppression or renunciation of instincts and particularly of aggression. The suppressing of the external expression of aggression allows it to become internalized as fear of loss of love and as conscience. Thus, as culture evolves, more suppression of aggression is needed and more guilt is generated, experienced as malaise and unhappiness. The present book considers the suppression of direct expression of aggression in relation to the influence of complex organizational structures, a subject to which Freud made no explicit reference. It is argued here that the suppression of direct aggression and the emergence of non-confrontational camouflaged aggression are part of the same process, and, from a Freudian perspective, camouflaged aggression can increase guilt. Freud noted that religions tend to both exploit and alleviate this sense of guilt. By extension, I would add the speculation that modern society, in interest of alleviating guilt, is producing more guilt-free individuals: psychopaths.

In summary, I suggest three sources of discontent resulting from the expansion of formal structures and complex systems. The first is an increase in camouflaged aggression; the second is an increase in self-directed aggression; and the third is the increase in the ratio of negative feedback to positive feedback, thus contributing to depression. Accordingly, the organizational individual—that is, all of us—is likely to be increasingly victimized by aggression delivered by others, by self, and by the imbalance between positive and negative feedback.

CAMOUFLAGED AGGRESSION
AND PERSONALITY

ANYONE IS CAPABLE of engaging in camouflaged aggression within an environment conducive to its expression, particularly one in which such behaviour is normative. However, it is not possible to fully understand any setting which involves prolonged interaction among individuals without consideration of the personalities of those individuals who comprise its social milieu. Whether and how an individual expresses aggression in any situation is determined by the interaction between that environment and the individual's personality: the relatively enduring characteristics of the individual.

Structural sociology theory (e.g., Marxist theories; the social strain theory of Merton, 1968) has promoted a conception of human nature that grossly underemphasizes the role of individual personality factors. This theory also ignores the role of intentionality, reducing it to a mere possibility within the social context. Such emphasis on structure at the expense of process was referred to by Wrong (1961) as the "over-socialized" conception of human beings. This conception denies that human beings are active agents who each bring specific biographies, perspectives, and dispositions with them to the environments in which they interact. These specific factors lead them to act in different ways within the same social context. An adequate model of human interaction in organizations must synthesize environmental and personality factors and adopt a psychosocial perspective. How people function in any social setting is a function of the interaction of personality and circumstance. It should be further stressed here that personality is not a mere constellation of inclinations, preferences, and tastes acquired in the course of development. Personality is fundamentally rooted in one's brain structures, physiology, and genetic inheritance. Advanced medical imaging is now revealing that all types of mental illness and personality disorders, and many forms of social and sexual deviance, evidence certain brain damages or abnormal brain functioning.

A psychosocial perspective is also essential to an understanding of how aggression is expressed (or suppressed) in organizations. In the case of camouflaged aggression, the interaction between organizational structures and personality, particularly disordered personality, is expected to be influenced by two main processes:

1. *Quantity to quality conversion.* Erich Fromm (1955) argued that the character and functioning of organizations can be strongly influenced by the preponderance of certain personality types within them. This phenomenon is propagated by a process of recruitment whereby members of management seek to hire individuals who resemble them in personality style. As a result, an increase in the number of individuals possessing a certain personality trait or orientation yields an alteration in the nature of the organization; quantity converts to quality. For example, having more than one manager with a paranoid personality orientation may lead to the development of excessive surveillance and supervision, which may in turn lead to the hiring of more security-oriented managers.

2. *Personality-job fit.* The organizational research dealing with the compatibility between the characteristics of personality and job is extensive. The *personality-job fit theory* (see, e.g., Caplan, 1987)

postulates that the closer the traits between the person and the job, the higher the chance of workplace productivity and satisfaction. The personality-job fit would imply a match between predominantly positive (prosocial) characteristics belonging to both the individual and the job. But there are cases where this fit is between antisocial traits of the worker and the job structures. Perhaps the word "marriage" would be symbolically more appropriate in this context than the word "fit," since marriage can involve disharmony and schism in the midst of a cooperative unity. There is always the possibility of an adaptive match between negative personality traits and the structures of the position. An example of this match is the compatibility and adaptiveness of a passive-aggressive style to complex hierarchical structures. This compatibility enhances the motivation of such an incumbent to aggress and to avail him- or herself of all available opportunities for that purpose. As a result, camouflaged aggression is likely to resonate and thrive around such incumbents. The organization may well founder under the force of myriad rules and procedures which appear benign but owe their development to the aggressive needs of disordered personalities placed in certain positions. An onlooker might attribute the resultant deterioration of the organization to its excessive bureaucratization, whereas the real source of the problem is to be found, not in bureaucratic procedures per se, but in the psycho-structural fit between the position's structures and the personality of certain incumbents.

The view that humans are abstract generalized sociocultural entities is rejected from the perspective of this text in favour of an interactive one which stresses that the socialization of people into a social system is never entirely successful and that no social system is immune to the aberrations of personality or brain disorders.

Camouflaged Aggression and Personality Disorders

The category of personality disorders is a broad one. It includes behaviour problems that differ greatly in form and severity. Some individuals exhibit extremely unethical or criminal behaviour and are unable to function in a normal setting; many of them are incarcerated in prisons or secure psychiatric hospitals. Others function adequately and may be highly successful in their careers but have deeply imbedded and long-standing antisocial personality traits that make them troublesome or difficult to get along with and cause problems for themselves and others in social or occupational situations.

There are ten personality disorders diagnosed according to their most prominent behavioural characteristics (American Psychiatric Association, 2013). These disorders all evidence a persistent interpersonal conduct leading to fractured relationships and causing considerable suffering to those with whom they come in contact. An organization whose membership includes individuals with any of the personality disorders described in this chapter can be crippled by the impact of such individuals on the way aggression is expressed within that organization. Such individuals may achieve positions of considerable influence in organizations in spite of their personality disorders or possibly because of them. The influence of even one such individual can be staggering.

In order to identify the organizational features of personality disorders it may be useful to distinguish them from other psychiatric disorders with which they are often confused. There are three broad categories of abnormal behaviour.

a. *Psychosis*: disorders characterized by a severe rift with reality, associated with delusions, hallucinations, and/or extreme changes in mood. Psychosis is seen in those with schizophrenia, psychotic paranoia, and affective disorders (including bipolar disorder and psychotic depression).

b. *Psychoneurosis*: disorders in which there is no loss of contact with reality but the individual's efficiency may be impaired by anxiety, guilt, depression, or fear. Symptoms may include phobia, hypochondria, obsessive-compulsiveness, psychogenic pain, panic attacks, excessive tension, inhibition, psychological conflicts, and ambivalence.

c. *Personality disorders*: disorders that present, to a certain extent, the converse of psychoneurosis. Reduced, rather than excessive, anxiety predominates, and conflicts are acted out on others rather than against self. These disorders are essentially interpersonal ones; they are also more resistant to change and modification than are neuroses.

Since the turn of the twentieth century, much clinical interest and research has been devoted to the study of psychoses and psychoneuroses. Much less medical and academic research and theorizing has occurred in the case of personality disorders. Research attention to personality disorders has been relatively meagre and surprisingly late in blooming. For example, serious research on psychopathy started to take place only in the late 1970s, over thirty years after the publication of Harvey Cleckley's *Mask of Sanity* in 1941, a work which provided a comprehensive clinical profile of the psychopath. This disparity in the volume of research could be explained by the fact that psychotics are more accessible to professionals because the generally debilitative effects of these conditions require long-term psychiatric supervision. In the case of neuroses, individuals themselves often seek professional help in order to alleviate distressing symptoms. In personality disorders, these conditions seldom apply. Individuals with personality disorders do not suffer from manifest impairments of their rational faculties or of their everyday functioning. They also seldom experience personal distress or a need for symptom alleviation or self-improvement. Accordingly, such individuals are less likely to come under the scrutiny of professionals.

Psychotic or psychoneurotic individuals can create many problems in organizations, but organizations are particularly vulnerable to the destructive behaviour of individuals with personality disorders. They will be the focus of this chapter.

Personality Disorders

The essential feature of a personality disorder is an enduring pattern of behaviour that is maladaptive for the individual but even more damaging to others. Although there may be no manifestation of the symptoms, such as distorted perception of reality, or excessive anxiety, tension, or fears, the individual evidences persistent problems in interpersonal and occupational functioning. In fact, in contrast to the neurotic personality, individuals with personality disorders evidence a relative absence of anxiety, tension, fear, or guilt and seem to be little constrained by conscience. Their lack of conscience enables them to act out their frustrations and conflicts on others with minimal self-restraint. The individual with a personality disorder is self-centred, projects fault and blame for the problems they create onto others, and seldom evidence self-criticism or a need for change. They usually possess an exceptional ability for deception and for masking their ego-centred motives. Because of their egocentricity and the fluidity of their conscience, the interpersonal behaviour of the individual with a personality disorder is little influenced by the internal controls of personal responsibility. External controls are required to curtail their interpersonally damaging behaviour. Personality disorders share a common psychological substrate in terms of failed separation-individuation, lack of object constancy, and a defective superego. Personality disorders also share reliance on primitive defences such as splitting, projective identification, denial, primitive idealization, omnipotence, and devaluation, which differ from those defences used at a higher level of character organization (e.g., repression, reaction formation, conversion, and displacement).

The impact of neurotic disorders on the quality of interpersonal interaction tends to be far less negative than that of personality disorders. In the case of the neurotics, with some exceptions, they tend to do more damage to themselves and their closest associates than to others. In organizations they are most likely to evidence personal distress and inefficiency or limited productivity. They may be subject to frequent minor illnesses, perfectionism, workaholism, absenteeism, and vulnerability to interpersonal conflicts. The social and organizational damage created by individuals with personality disorders is usually much more drastic. They can undermine the entire social fabric of stable, reciprocal, and socially responsible relationships and the efficient functioning of the organization.

The clinical profiles of these disorders presented below are based on the third revised edition (DSM III-R, 1987) and the fourth and fifth editions (DSM-IV, 1994; DSM-V, 2013) of the *Diagnostic and Statistical Manual of Mental Disorders* of the American Psychiatric Association. The following are brief descriptions of the profiles and my observations regarding the contribution of personality disorders to camouflaged aggression in organizations. The reference to psychiatric diagnosis provides standard models for identifying the elusive behaviour.

Passive-Aggressive Personality Disorder

An individual with this disorder is typically fixated on expressing aggression in indirect and non-confrontational ways. The non-confrontational expression and the individual's reluctance to explicitly identify the problem leave others feeling frustrated and distressed. These individuals make their associates suffer through apparently non-aggressive, yet exasperating, behaviours such as pouting, procrastination, stubbornness, and deliberate inefficiency; they can be annoyingly polite, too understanding, excessively apologetic, or overly helpful—in ways which turn out to have effects opposite to those which the individual apparently intended. Also, common to those with this disorder is careful planning (or plotting) in which, while appearing to be doing their duty or trying to help people or the organization itself, they embarrass others by disseminating harmful information, make themselves unavailable when most needed, or create enmity among friends and discord among cooperating groups. Frequent targets are individuals who have some power over them, such as spouses or bosses, whom they cannot or will not confront.

Within the organization, people with this personality disorder can be much more destructive than in their home or among their circle of friends, settings where their behaviour can more easily be recognized. The structures in organizations provide innumerable opportunities for non-confrontational delivery and the masking of aggression; these structures enable the passive-aggressive individual to mask his or her aggressiveness behind a cloak of respectability. Those with this personality disorder are always on the lookout for personal vulnerabilities of coworkers, and for situations where members of the organization find themselves in compromised conditions, so that they can embarrass or blackmail them. Because the victims often do not know that the aggressor has intended to harm them, they have no clear target, no one against whom they can justifiably express retaliatory aggression. As a result, individuals with this disorder tend to increase the quantum of aggression within the organization through their tendency to both initiate and prolong camouflaged aggression.

Paranoid Personality Disorder

The essential feature of this disorder is a tendency to misinterpret the actions of people as deliberately demeaning or threatening. Those with the disorder evidence a generalized suspicion and expectation of being exploited, plotted against, or harmed by others in some way. Frequently a person with this disorder will question, without justification, the loyalty or trustworthiness of friends or associates. They may be reluctant to confide in others because of a fear that the information will be used against them. Often such individuals are easily slighted and quick to react with anger or counterattack, and are often hypervigilant to perceived threat. They tend to hold grudges for a long time, and seldom forgive slights, insults, or injuries.

When individuals with this disorder find themselves in a new situation, they intensely and narrowly search for confirmation of their expectations, with little appreciation of the total context. They are usually argumentative and exaggerate difficulties, "making mountains out of molehills." Such an individual can readily escalate a benign discussion into an argument with a contradictory and hostile attitude. They are very critical of others but have great difficulty in accepting blame or criticism themselves. They tend to be overserious and lack a sense of humour. They tend to be rigid and unwilling to compromise and may generate uneasiness and fear in others. Individuals with this disorder are keenly aware of power and rank and of who is superior or inferior, and are often envious of those in positions of power. They are aloof, with a hostile distancing of themselves from others, and are contemptuous of people they see as weak, soft, or sickly.

Unlike individuals with some of the other personality disorders, the paranoid person appears to have no redeeming social quality, such as the charm and affability often presented by psychopathic, narcissistic, and histrionic personalities, or the initially polite and smooth demeanour of the passive-aggressive. Most of the interactive dimensions of the paranoid personality disorder are usually unappealing and problematic.

Because those with the disorder are continually suspicious of others and on guard against possible attack, they create many conflicts within the workplace through their misinterpretation of people's motives. Their propensity to exaggerate threats or challenges and to counterattack tends to escalate simple conflicts and augment aggression within the organization. Their overcritical attitude toward others, and their argumentative and belligerent style, tend to deter disagreement with them, a condition that motivates camouflaging or displacing aggression.

Unlike passive-aggressive individuals, who restrain their aggression when faced with an explicit retaliatory threat, those with paranoid personalities regroup psychologically and then counterattack in a manner that often escalates conflict and hostility. Their tendency to be moralistic, grandiose, and punitive may motivate some of them to embark on vigilant crusades against individuals or groups, thus sowing animosities and divisiveness within the organization.

I have frequently observed alliances between individuals who share this personality trait. Two individuals with this disorder may team up under the paranoid "ideology" of suspiciousness and contempt for others, and through a mutually resonating moralistic campaign of vigilance and scheming. Tobak (1989) observed the frequent coexistence of expedient mendacity and moralistic self-righteousness in the paranoid character. In short, individuals with paranoid personality disorders are prolific producers and amplifiers of conflicts, and can be major contributors to the quantum of aggression within the organization.

Narcissistic Personality Disorder

Individuals with this disorder are typically preoccupied with cultivating a grandiose image of themselves. They are driven to maintain this image of self-importance through constantly seeking attention and admiration from others. They are hypersensitive to criticism, arrogant, power-seeking, self-centred, manipulative, and imbued with a profound degree of entitlement that places their wishes above legal or ethical limits. This disorder, sometimes referred to as *social malignancy*, is evidencing marked increase in present-day societies, taking a heavy toll on the quality of social life.

The following are their primary characteristics:

1. *Grandiosity*. They have an inflated sense of self-importance and superiority (e.g., they exaggerate their talents and achievements) and expect to be noticed and treated as "special." They entertain

grandiose fantasies of unlimited success and a belief in their invulnerability, self-sufficiency, and uniqueness. At the same time, they are referential, boastful, and pretentious.

2. *Problematic Interpersonal Relations.* They require constant attention and admiration, (e.g., they may keep fishing for compliments). They have a sense of entitlement: an unreasonable expectation of favourable treatment or a tendency to disregard or circumvent legal and ethical considerations while pursuing their goals. They often are interpersonally exploitative and manipulative, taking advantage of others to achieve their own ends. They feel threatened by goodness in others and defend against envy by devaluating, attempting to control, or avoiding contact with them altogether.

3. *Reactiveness.* When these individuals fail to obtain what they want or are subjected to criticism, they often react with rage and vindictiveness or shame and humiliation. Failure is perceived as an extreme personal threat, which can lead to vindictiveness, or to suicidal ideation and other self-destructive reactions. An unresponsive or unsupportive environment can lead them to experience transient mood states such as emptiness, boredom, and meaninglessness.

4. *Lack of Social and Moral Conscience.* Such individuals tend to be highly ambitious and achievement motivated. They are self-centred and uncommitted to anyone; all goals and espoused notions and beliefs are upheld only in the service of self or self-image. They can be skilful and charming manipulators who have no genuine regard for values or rules. Their social history often reveals sexual promiscuity and antisocial behaviour.

Malignant Narcissism

This term was introduced by Otto Kernberg in 1984. He used it to describe a toxic combination of grandiose and sadistic strivings that develops in some narcissists. Kernberg outlined four features of this syndrome: 1) a typical narcissistic personality disorder, 2) antisocial behaviour, 3) sadism, and 4) a deeply paranoid orientation toward life. Individuals with malignant narcissism consistently attempt to destroy, symbolically castrate, and dehumanize others. These traits are often expressed through ideology by leaders of religious cults and extremist political groups. The leaders may display concern and loyalty to their peers and followers, something that distinguishes them from the psychopathic personality proper. Malignant narcissists' paranoid tendencies are manifested in their viewing of others as enemies or fools and in their preoccupation with conspiracies.

Kernberg did not focus on the external factors that may accelerate the development to malignant narcissism. I think that a speedy acquisition of administrative or political power and of wealth can transform mild pathological narcissism into a malignant one. I have observed cases involving a rapid transition from a mild narcissistic orientation toward a malignant one after individuals acquire substantial wealth or a position of power.

An Oncological Model of Narcissism

In 1993 I submitted a research paper with the above title to the Research Division of the Ministry of the Solicitor General of Canada. The model accounts for the development of narcissism from simple exhibitionism to malignant narcissism through a process of alienation of self-image. In young people an early overinvestment in body image or in the attention of an audience involves a level of alienation (splitting) of self-image from self. Narcissus first fell in love with the image of himself in the water and not with himself. Alienation here adopts the Hegelian definition wherein an aspect of the self becomes externalized and objectified and this causes it to become alienated or split from, and thus to negatively target, the person. As the alienated self-image become socially objectified it requires more energy from the individual to maintain and protect its grandiosity. While the healthy self-image protects the individual's normal social functioning, the alienated self-image extols energy from the individual to promote and defend it.

Freud (1920/1948) described the cancer cell as narcissistic. The parallelism of the alienated self-image to the cancer cell is striking. The cancer cell initially disengages from its biological context and assumes a self-centred existence. As it continues to grow it becomes a tumour that can disrupt the functioning of body fluids, tissues, and organs. Thus, in an individual, narcissistic malignancy starts with exhibitionism (mild alienation of self-image) and can progress to pathological narcissism (a "tumorous" self-image), which forces the individual to engage in antisocial behaviour in order to carry on. This model draws attention to the dangers of encouraging a culture of exhibitionism, one that is largely enabled, especially among young people, by means of electronic imagery. Exhibitionism can initiate a process of alienation of self-image, leading to pathological and malignant narcissism. In order to maintain the grandiosity of the self, the narcissist needs to constantly supply his or her image with the attention and reactions of others and at heavy personal and social cost. This dependency on eliciting the attention and reaction of others moves this disorder from interpersonal to social pathology.

Narcissistic personality disorder clearly takes a heavy toll on the organization. However, two traits that are typically characteristic of individuals with this disorder are particularly dangerous for organizations. They are an elevated sense of *entitlement* and a deployment of the *splitting* mechanism.

Individuals with this disorder believe their feelings and their wishes are both legitimate and justified. Accordingly, they feel entitled to use anything at their disposal, or any person, to realize those wishes. The interests of the organization are often the victims of this sense of entitlement.

Splitting, which is a mechanism common to all personality disorders, essentially involves a separation of a feeling or a relationship from its context. For example, a simple disagreement may suffice to make the narcissist react with overwhelming contempt and animosity to a partner with whom he or she has had a long-standing relationship. The trusted friend and partner can become an enemy who is hated absolutely and eternally. What such a victim finds most shocking is that all of the long-standing history of cooperative and friendly relations suddenly becomes of no significance. It is as if the other party has no memory of the relationship. Through this splitting mechanism, the narcissist can suddenly and radically shift allegiance. A trusted friend can become an enemy; the partner may become an adversary; a colleague who previously was viewed with the deepest respect may come to be viewed with unqualified contempt. The converse process is also true, such as idealizing a previously despised person.

The organization itself can become a victim of the same pathological process: a virtual pawn of the narcissist's perverse sense of entitlement and splitting. An individual with this disorder can turn on the organization and bring it down even if he or she had heretofore worked tirelessly over many years for it. In a spiteful and grandiose finale, the narcissist would communicate the message, "I created you and now I am going to destroy you."

The Narcissistic Principle of Equivalence

In my investigations of this disorder in the organizational context, I was able to observe another dynamic related to the splitting mechanism. This type of individual can spontaneously and with remarkable ease work for a certain project and against it at the same time. He or she can be geared, psychologically, equally toward both the promotion and the demise of a worthy project. If the individual expects to reap benefits, and particularly prestige, from supporting the venture, he or she will be all for it. If that forthcoming prestige runs the risk of being shared by others, or if the thwarting of the venture can be attributed mainly to his or her own doing, then he or she will mobilize against it and seek to destroy it. Thus, it is the potential of ego-aggrandizement that determines the direction of the commitment rather than the intrinsic social value of the collective venture. Rationalizations are employed in either direction. It is intriguing how the narcissistic ego-centredness can neutralize the oppositional relationship between construction and destruction. I call this proclivity the *narcissistic principle of equivalence*. The above paragraph from the first edition of this book has been quoted online (in a Wikipedia article) and has provoked considerable interest. An assumption was made that I wrote a book on the subject entitled *The Narcissistic Principle of Equivalence*; although that is not the case, the interest generated indicates the need for more research into this clinical dynamic of narcissism.

Not too long ago, I conducted a seminar in organizational behaviour with a group of bankers. In the seminar, cases of financial collapse of specific companies were analyzed, with particular emphasis on the personality profile of the major player. It was a surprise to most participants when they came to realize that the collapse of some of these companies appeared to have been the product of irrational decisions on the part of a key director rather the result of financial or market conditions. What lies behind many fatal business decisions is not just a lack of business savvy or unfortunate timing or global economic factors but the malignant aggression of an enraged narcissist. Unrecognized and/or uncontrolled pathological narcissism can produce organizational collapse.

Antisocial Personality Disorder—the Psychopath

"Antisocial personality disorder" is the term now used to refer to the psychopathic personality. Harvey Cleckley presented a comprehensive clinical profile of the psychopath in the first edition of *The Mask of Sanity* (1941), a work he continued to refine to its fifth edition (1976). The individuals in his case studies evidence few of the symptoms of mental illness, such as lack of contact with reality, delusions, or anxiety, but persist in aberrant antisocial behaviour. Cleckley described the clinical profile of the psychopath in terms of sixteen characteristics, abridged briefly to the following:

1. Egocentrism: self-gratifying, hedonistic, with lack of empathy or concern for others;
2. An absence of conscience, moral or ethical values, guilt, or remorse;
3. Lack of love and attachment to individuals, institutions, places, or ideas;
4. An ability to deceive and manipulate people, with use of masking, lying, mimicking, rationalizing, charm, and charisma;
5. Impulsivity, poor behaviour controls, and inability to follow a life plan;
6. A life history of antisocial behaviour.

The most salient behavioural features of psychopaths are inadequate development of conscience and lack of anxiety and guilt. They may be able to verbalize their understanding of moral values, but it is often shallow, and the allegiance they may express to social values is usually not borne out by their behaviour. Even when they are caught engaging in unacceptable behaviour, they are devoid of feelings of remorse, shame, or guilt. Little consideration is given to the effects of their actions on other people. However, even though psychopaths are essentially amoral, their ability to impress, charm, manipulate, and exploit others enables them not only to take advantage of them but also to do so without raising suspicion or getting caught. Even when caught they may seem to be sincerely repentant and are often quickly forgiven, as they use their humour and charm and ability to rationalize their behaviour to appease people. Although they are highly egocentric, they seem to have good insight into other people's needs and weaknesses and are adept at winning their confidence and then exploiting them. Although they are able to win the admiration and support of other people, anti-social personalities are seldom able to make close friends because they are egocentric, nonempathetic, and unable to experience or understand allegiance or love.

Systematic empirical research of this disorder (see, e.g., Hare, 1970; Hare & Schalling, 1978; Lykken, 1995) indicates that the disorder is associated with autonomic under-arousal and cortical immaturity; thus physiological under-stimulation might help to explain the psychopath's quest for excitement, lack of anxiety, and failure to be influenced by threats of impending punishment. In fact, when psychopaths arrive, toward old age, at the "burned-out" stage that evidences a decrease in antisocial behaviour, their autonomic and brain patterns start changing toward normal readings. Recently developed brain imagery reveals certain abnormalities in the brains of psychopaths.

The literature suggests that, given their impulsivity, need for excitement, and a tendency for immediate gratification, psychopaths are seldom attracted to or capable of maintaining organizational careers. However, this may be true only for the more extreme cases who come to the attention of the authorities, that is, those whose antisocial behaviour leads to their involvement in criminal activities. Many psychopaths are well-educated, sophisticated achievers who are able to use their manipulative skills and charm to obtain powerful positions despite their lack of genuine allegiance to individuals or institutions. Such "successful" psychopaths have a profile that is very similar to that of the extreme narcissistic disorder, and, in some cases, is almost indistinguishable. Many psychopaths are confined in correctional institutions, but most manage to escape incarceration or even detection and prosecution, even though they frequently engage in immoral and criminal ventures. Psychopaths can be found in every field of endeavour—in business, in universities, in schools, and in churches. Many of them are never convicted of any crime. They may be functioning as lawyers, doctors, executives, professors, or politicians. They are just as likely to be found working in businesses, government offices, and professions as they are to be found in prisons.

The alarm regarding the existence of an "adequate" or "successful" psychopath was sounded as early as 1957 by Norman Mailer. In an essay published in *Dissent Magazine*, Mailer prophesied that the psychopathic personality could become the central expression of human nature before the twentieth century is over. He suggested that our culture is increasingly being influenced by psychopaths as the condition of psychopathy is present in a host of high-profile individuals, including politicians, newspaper columnists, entertainers, and "half the executives of Hollywood, television and advertising" (p. 282).

Fifteen years later, Harrington (1972), a writer and a journalist, set out to reassess the above thesis; his findings were presented in a book containing observations, interviews, and descriptions of psychopathic individuals from all walks of life. His conclusion was that "psychopathy as illness and style have now merged. You can hardly, if at all, tell [psychopaths] apart any more" (p. 198). In response to Harrington, Cleckley (1976), in his fifth edition of *The Mask of Sanity*, confirmed the omnipresence of successful psychopaths and provided descriptions of psychopathic professionals, including one who was a psychiatrist.

Manipulative behaviour exhibited by the average individual was studied by Christie and Geis (1970), and the findings were discussed under the topic of Machiavellianism. The authors developed a measure to assess this interpersonal style and formulated the following four-feature profile of the Machiavel: 1) a relative lack of affect in interpersonal relations and the viewing of others as objects for manipulation; 2) a lack of concern with conventional morality; 3) a lack of gross psychopathology; 4) a low ideological commitment—more interest in tactics to a utilitarian end rather than striving for an idealistic goal. The Machiavel profile can be viewed as a "satellite" of the psychopath. Hare (1991) developed a "Psychopathic Check List," which can be filled out by persons who know the individual.

Psychopathic behaviour can be learned through having to adapt to socially unstable family or environmental conditions or through association with psychopathic models. Harrington's (1972) suggestion that psychopathology can progress from a personality style to an ethic was later echoed by Lasch (1979), who claimed that narcissistic behaviour has become an accepted and normative style of social interaction. "Adequate" psychopaths not only create interpersonal conflict within organizations by their devious antisocial and manipulative behaviour, they also promote the attitude that egocentricity, manipulation, and deceit are effective, and acceptable, forms of interpersonal conduct. In summary, the psychopath can undermine the values of the organization and its members.

Histrionic Personality Disorder

The essential feature of this disorder is immaturity, emotional insta-bility, pervasive and excessive emotionality, and attention-seeking behaviour. Individuals with this disorder are self-centred, vain, and uncomfortable when they are not the centre of attention. If ignored, they may do something dramatic to draw the focus of attention to themselves. These individuals are often over-reactive and inappro-priately sexually provocative or seductive. They are overly concerned with impressing others and may spend excessive time and money on grooming and clothes and surrounding themselves with the trappings of success. Individuals with this disorder often have a style of speech that is unfocused, lacking in detail, and theatrical.

In seeking to gain approval, histrionics resemble individuals with a narcissistic personality disorder. However, they usually have weaker egos, and hence exhibit emotional volatility and poor ability to consolidate power. They are suggestible, oversensitive to criticism, and tend to consider relationships to be more intimate than they actually are. Their seductive style can lead to unwarranted sexual advances. Although they often initiate a job or project with great enthusiasm, their interest dissipates quickly. They are often frustrated by situations that involve delayed gratification. Long-term relationships may be neglected to make way for the excitement of new ones. The interpersonal relationships of such individuals are usually stormy and continuously generate tensions and conflicts in the workplace.

Obsessive-Compulsive Personality Disorder

The essential features of the obsessive-compulsive personality disorder are a preoccupation with orderliness, perfectionism, and control at the expense of flexibility, openness, and efficiency. Individuals with this disorder seek to maintain a sense of control over themselves and others through painstaking attention to rules, trivial details, procedures, lists, schedules, or forms to the extent that the major purpose of the activity is lost. Their perfectionism and preoccupation with trivia tend to interfere with their management of time and with task completion. They may be excessively devoted to work and productivity to the exclusion of leisure activities and friendships. They are over conscientious, scrupulous, and inflexible about matters of morality, ethics, and procedure. They tend to adopt a miserly spending style toward self and others; money is viewed as something to be hoarded, not spent or invested. They evidence rigidity and stubbornness in most contexts and are reluctant to delegate tasks or work to others unless the delegate conforms precisely to the compulsive's procedures.

The behaviour patterns associated with this disorder are similar to those of the neurotic suffering from obsessive-compulsive symptoms. In the case of neurotics, they often experience undesired thoughts (obsessions) and actions (compulsions) as a source of extreme anxiety; they recognize that these thoughts and actions are irrational but they cannot control them. Individuals with obsessive-compulsive personality disorder, on the other hand, may be anxious about getting all their work done in keeping with their exacting standards but are not anxious about their compulsiveness itself. They appear to be oblivious to the fact that their style can be problematic and that other people can be distressed by it.

The organizational implications of this personality style are obvious. The rigidity, stubbornness, and morbid clinging to procedure can generate frustration, stagnation, and demoralization.

Avoidant Personality Disorder

Individuals with this disorder are hypersensitive to rejection, criticism, and ridicule. They are too fearful of potential rejection to seek out others, voice opinions, or take positions. Their everyday interpersonal relations are often very limited, partly because they avoid interactions and partly because their excessive passivity makes them unattractive to others. They may be able to cope reasonably well within structured work relationships without major conflicts. However, in organizations they can indirectly generate a great deal of aggression. Their passivity and unassertiveness tend to create a point of least resistance which attracts aggression both toward them and toward people working with them. Moreover, the non-confrontational and indecisive behaviour of these individuals handicaps their ability to contain the aggressiveness of employees working with them or to protect those working under them. Thus, by attracting and by failing to contain aggression, they serve to catalyse and augment it within the organization.

There are three remaining personality disorders. *Borderline personality disorder* manifests mood instability, identity disturbance, and weak ego. *Schizoid personality disorder* is characterized by social avoidance and a lack of the social skills needed to form social relations. *Schizotypal personality disorder* is typical of the person who is seclusive and eccentric in communication and behaviour, and resorts to highly personalized and superstitious thinking. These three personality disorders have in common weak ego organization, poor interpersonal skills, and personal styles that are persistent and socially inadequate.

According to Stone (1993) prominent narcissistic traits can coexist with any of the personality disorders. My observations concur with those of Stone; whenever a configuration of a personality disorder was identified, a concomitant measure of pathological narcissism was also present. It appears that pathological narcissism (involving extreme self-centredness) is an underlying feature of all such disorders, and perhaps this is what gives personality disorders the distinction of social malignancy. Also, more than one disorder can coexist in the same person, allowing shifting among different behavioural axes. Researching the impact of personality disorders in organizations is best carried out within normal work conditions. Some of the novel constructs suggested in this book may be useful in motivating and guiding subsequent systematic research.

A Case of General Relevance

One interesting field observation was relayed to me by a political veteran active in the 1960s in Lebanon. He described the profile of individuals from Marxist political groups who undertook the tasks of infiltrating certain charitable organizations. Their goal was either to wreck and dismantle such organizations or to dominate them and keep them in a weakened state—leaving them half dead. These under-takings were ideologically justified by the notion that these social organizations were bourgeoisie-serving entities or impediments to the coming "revolution." The infiltrators were self-recruited and evidenced pronounced inclinations toward paranoid conspiratorial thinking and Machiavellianism. The ideological sanctioning of their camouflaged aggression neutralized any guilt or ambivalence associated with the mission and allowed them to enthusiastically indulge their personal pathologies. My acquaintance described the heightened excitement, thrill, and enthusiasm which accompanied their scheming. What he recalls most vividly was the "smile"—an exuberant, complacent, congratulatory, and self-assured smile they exchanged when they met to review operations. When I explained to my acquaintance the previ-ously described idea of the psycho-structural fit (the "psycho-structural marriage"), he exclaimed: "but of course...even their incompetence was happily married." Apparently, in cases where the infiltrators managed to take over as the directors of some of these associations, they did not have the adequate organizational skills to manage them. Thus, their original goal of crippling the organization resonated with their lack of skills and with the least-effort principle. I think that there is further need for research focusing on such adaptations involving pathological personality proclivities and organizational roles and structures— adaptations that are psychologically functional for the incumbent but dysfunctional to the organization.

Camouflaged Aggression in "Normal" Personality Profiles

As suggested before, camouflaged aggression may be planned and carried out by normal people striving to achieve a goal. A specific goal can force them to engage in deception, with the expectation that such behaviour be abandoned when the project ends. It is also expected that normal personality functioning (in terms of ethicality, conscience, humanity) will ultimately exert a form of control over the Machiavellianism and harmful manipulation they may have adopted. There are also individuals with normal personality functioning who evidence traits that are socially accepted, and at times admired, but can have a harmful impact when expressed within an organization. I have developed elsewhere (Abdennur, 1987, 2014) three personality profiles, each considered within the range of normal, yet capable of causing social damage: *conflict avoidance, conflict reconciliation*, and *anti-organizational*. All can create a syndrome of traits with problematic social and political implications.

Conflict Avoidance as a Personality Profile

Unlike generalized avoidant behaviour found in the avoidant personality disorder, avoidance in this profile is largely confined to conflict. A persistent effort to avoid conflict can be the result of an inability to psychologically cope with it, although this behaviour may be considered normal and is often admired. However, since conflict and its resolution are part of daily social living, deficiencies in the ability to deal adequately with conflict can have problematic social consequences. The tendency to continually avoid confrontation is seen as a function of a weak ego; it can be aggravated by social norms that encourage conflict-avoidant types of resolutions, or by the lack of organizational avenues for the expression of direct aggression. In a book solely dedicated to conflict avoidance (Abdennur, 1987), I proposed that avoidance can permeate many domains of personality, forming a syndrome. This personality syndrome can impact social and political institutions in a negative manner.

A tendency to avoid conflict or confrontation can be generalized throughout various aspects of personality; I label this tendency the *conflict avoidance syndrome.* My research (Abdennur, 1987) found conflict avoidance choices and preferences to be consistent throughout many domains of an individual's functioning: perceptual, cognitive, psychodynamic, aesthetic, recreational, and political. The traits identified within the conflict avoidance syndrome are excessive fear of violent aggression, concreteness, exhibitionism and theatricality, teleological preoccupations, and the resort to spiritualized-metaphorical (non-abstract) thinking. The reliance on these traits helps the individual to avoid or minimize conflict.

A major impact of a conflict avoidance orientation is that it reduces the possibility of achieving adequate solutions to problems because it leads the individual to avoid prompt, decisive, or radical action. Procrastination, concessions, and compromises tend to prevail, and expediency is often substituted for principle. Individuals with this orientation can also distort problems and issues in order to accommodate them within their conflict-avoidant methods of intervention. For example, the plight of children in some developing countries is operationally defined, by those with such personalities, as an issue to be addressed by charitable relief and sponsorship of children by families in the West. While such intervention can be helpful in some cases, it leaves the causes of the problem (e.g., population control, income inequality) unaddressed. One of the most devastating blows to the natural environment was perpetrated by groups of individuals with this personality type. The exhibitionist and ineffective methods of these environmental activists included noisy demonstrations, marches, candle vigils, body painting, placards, climbing of chimneys, media stunts, and grand-standing in striving to "inform the public." The ineffectiveness of their actions is demonstrated in their failure to stop major environmental threats such as the development of the tar sands in Alberta, the clear-cutting of forests in Northern Ontario, and the resort to the highly polluting fracking method in the midst of plentiful oil and gas supplies. Protecting the environment is a grave and radical challenge, one that these conflict avoiders are incapable of meeting. Their media-based exhibitionistic approaches may have perpetrated another social damage, namely, the displacement individuals who might otherwise have been capable of more effective intervention.

Another dangerous aspect of the conflict avoidance syndrome is that individuals seek to hire and recruit into organizations others with a similar orientation—those who will not rock the boat. Thus, conflict avoidants can come to predominate within an organization and thus influence its normative standards and approaches in a qualitative manner. Many social and political organizations have been rendered impotent by those who promote excessive accommodation and toler-ance. Conflict avoidants have been heavily recruited into the Canadian political and administrative systems, where they may have achieved institutional dominance. The excessive resort to unqualified tolerance and to pragmatic accommodation to social problems (e.g., the promo-tion of free-drug injection sites) in Canada may be encouraging a culture of moral relativism, banality, and oppressive liberalism.

In short, the impact of individuals with the conflict avoidance orien-tation on camouflaged aggression is aggravating in three ways. First, they are more in tune with passive and camouflaged aggression and are more likely to engage in it. Second, their pronounced non-confronta-tional behaviour precludes attempts at making conflicts explicit and the use of radical measures to end or contain them. Third, they constitute a non-confrontational matrix that allows a converse, and equally adverse, personality profile to perpetuate itself in management. That profile can be identified as a growing class of overtly aggressive, arrogantly intimidating, and self-serving managers. The unchallenging and passive disposition of conflict avoidants may allow the latter to thrive.

Conflict Reconciliation as a Personality Profile

The conflict reconciliation tendency is viewed as an essentially milder form of conflict avoidance, but one with different adaptation dynamics as dictated by the process of reconciliation. Identification of the traits associated with this type has been carried out analytically (Abdennur, 2014), based on the assumption that the three basic strategies in the adaptation to conflict (confrontation, conflict reconciliation, and conflict avoidance) constitute generalized and stable personality traits.

The conflict reconciler: 1) has an empirical epistemic style; 2) holds negotiation as the preferred method of conflict resolution; 3) focuses on concrete or operational items that can be used in negotiation; 4) seeks to arrive at a final deal or resolution; 5) turns the need to achieve reconciliation into an obsessive-compulsive need; and 6) operationalizes *issues* into *problems.*

The conceptualization of something as a *problem* is based on epistemological assumptions that a) *variables are part of a closed system,* like a machine where a malfunction can be identified and fixed; b) there exists *a previous state of normal functioning* that can be returned to after fixing the malfunction; c) *consensus on the need for intervention* is based on the conception of the cumulative effects of good acts; d) there is a *pressing need for immediate intervention*; and e) *radicalism exists at the concrete level,* that is, there is a need to fix the problem permanently. These assumptions implied in defining something as a problem can distort the comprehension of abstract and complex conditions.

Since the 1990s, there appears to have been an ever-greater need for negotiation and reconciliation at most organizational and political levels as a response to a growing need for stability within an increasingly interdependent world. The increased number of roles that demand conflict resolution has increased the demand for and recruitment of individuals who are psychologically adaptive to such roles. The advantages that can be reaped by the political-administrative system by having conflict reconcilers in authority positions may not be beneficial for society as whole.

Unlike the conflict-avoider personality profile, who verbalizes and "spiritualizes" intervention slogans, the conflict reconciler is more concrete and utilitarian. He or she can be ruthless with weaker opponents but submissive to those who are powerful. The proclivity for making deals causes the individual to fall into unending schemes and traps which dissipate energy, create only temporary solutions, and undermine principles. While the environment in the West was victimized by the approaches of the conflict avoidant, the conflict reconciler, in my view, has delivered devastating impacts to many Arab societies. The predominance of this deal-making type in Arab administration and political leadership has been responsible for the tolerance for dictators, the compromise of cultural integrity, and the demoralization of Arab populations.

An Anti-Organizational Personality Profile

The model proposed here identifies three personality traits that are to some extent contradictory but can become dynamically united within the same person. This convergence of traits seems to thrive in some business groups, particularly the self-employed, found in some developing countries characterized by mercantile economic activity, material prosperity, and global mobility. Although these traits are found within normally functioning individuals, their expression is particularly destructive to formal organizations.

1. Aggrandized Ego (Arrogant)
The individual possesses an expanded sense of self-worth and importance that may be rooted in several factors, such as a high level of narcissism, being part of a cohesive family or clan that tends to impart to the individual (often unrealistically) a sense of power and importance, or being the proprietor of a successful business in which there

are few outside constraints on decision-making. Success in business ventures further expands the individual's narcissistic sense of self-worth and entitlement, making him or her complacent toward his or her shortcomings.

2. Poor Intellectual Skills (Ignorant)

The individual suffers not from a lack of education but rather from the lack of a quality education. The inadequacy of the educational institutions or inadequate performance as student may result in in the individual's failure to grasp the basics of scientific methodology and critical reasoning. The individual may hold degrees, be a specialist in a certain field, converse in several languages, and be sophisticated in many technical domains, yet fail to develop an integrated body of knowledge. This condition may be aggravated when his or her early cultural milieu fails to instil a sense of authentic and integrated cultural identity.

Here we need to stress the distinction between intellectual and mental abilities. Intellectual ability moves across disciplines and fields of knowledge; it is an integration of specialized knowledge, personal experience, and basic methodology. Intellectual ability promotes reflection as opposed to impulsivity; it promotes the consideration of problems as issues; it refines social and political judgment; and it fosters a concern for rational and ethical consistency. The distinction between mental and intellectual skills has been further accentuated by the explosion of information and easy access to computer technology in recent decades. Abundantly available information is losing its previous knowledge status as the emphasis is shifting more toward the organization and integration of information. True knowledge has become closely tied to theory and method, and to the ability to come up with alternative models and perspectives rather than raw information. Thus, it is possible to be literate and overloaded with information but ignorant. Such intellectual ignorance promotes a commonsensical and utilitarian approach to social issues and undermines critical self-reflection. The individual does not read lengthy scholarly or academic books and his or her thinking remains concrete, intuitive, and pragmatic—characteristics that are inherently anti-intellectual.

3. Compromised Ethicality (Corrupt)

The individual lacks the norms that promote respect of time, respect for the reality and rights of interacting others, and respect for organizational demands. He or she also lacks a genuine feeling of responsibility for mistakes and holds a projective and self-serving view of reality. Briefly, his or her norms are fluid and self-centred, showing little regard for the greater social good.

Lacking an integrated knowledge of central issues, or having gaps in one's knowledge, usually promotes generalized feelings of doubt and hesitancy at the level of verbal and social expression. Also, when one harbours unethical designs or engages in an unethical enterprise, one is bound (unless one is a primary psychopath) to experience a certain degree of inhibition, guilt, or remorse. When the lack of ethicality and the absence of integrated knowledge become incorporated within a personality, they usually lower inner self-confidence and compromise assertiveness. In order to control this sense of guilt and diminished confidence, some individuals may resort to what in psychodynamics is called a "reaction formation," where there is a shift to feelings at the extreme opposite of the spectrum. Thus, instead of behaving timidly, an individual would act confidently, assertively, and boastfully. This behaviour is also seen as a compensatory reaction against the underlying guilt or feelings of inferiority. In this instance, therefore, the amicable, socially assertive, and confident style is essentially compensatory; it is propelled by weakness rather than by an abundance of strength, and this weakness readily betrays itself in the presence of stressful challenges. However, despite the preceding, I would suggest that the assertiveness of this three-trait profile is not compensatory. The three traits become autonomous and mutually reinforcing, creating a synergy. After being propelled by the force of narcissistic arrogance, intellectual constriction reinforces the lack of ethical scruples, with the three forming a powerful momentum.

Under the influence of this three-trait axis, the individual perceives the organization as an impediment, and in dealing with it he or she attempts to circumvent or manipulate its rules and employees for personal ends. Having an inherent disdain for corporate norms, and a narcissistic admiration for his or her own style, the individual resorts to bribery and other corrupt practices even if they are not needed. Methods of business operation are individualistic and non-corporate, and rely heavily on cultivating personal interactions with business contacts where the individual can wield influence with presents and favours. He or she can be seen as the typical anti-organizational personality. Certain socioeconomic conditions, such as the increasing reliance on self- or part-time employment, short-duration contracts, and communication technologies tend to move some individuals in the direction of solo enterprises and anti-corporate business practices.

Personality Disorders and Voluntary Organizations

Voluntary organizations differ from business or governmental ones in that their goals and membership are community-based; they are usually non-profit or charitable enterprises; they have less stringent formal structures and operate on limited volunteer time and limited budgets, often with funds raised through donations. These open and less binding features of voluntary associations can become highly attractive to individuals with personality disorders and particularly to the flamboyant types such as the narcissistic, psychopathic, paranoid, and histrionic personalities. A dialectical relationship, in fact, tends to exist between voluntary associations and individuals with personality disorders; they frequently initiate or supply the enthusiasm and energy for the sprouting of these associations but, at the same time, they embody the seeds of destruction and eventual demise of these very associations.

Voluntary associations are perceived by these persons as open pastures where their egos can graze on the attention and energy of the associations' members. These organizations are generally not sufficiently equipped to deal with them due to the voluntary and community nature of the enterprise, and this organizational vulnerability allows these individuals to perpetuate a chronic presence. When such persons become entrenched within the board of directors, they can lead to the collapse of these associations; more often, they cause their weakening, as volunteers, weary of the turmoil that has been generated, start to lose enthusiasm, pull out, or otherwise make themselves scarce. It should be noted that these disordered individuals may be entertaining and charismatic, and may volunteer for tasks with great dedication; however, when assessed over their total period of involvement, their negative input outweighs the positive.

The non-profit goals and less stringent organization of voluntary associations tend to encourage spontaneous and less masked self-expression. Accordingly, voluntary associations provide a convenient medium for the study of interactive patterns of various personality disorders. An area that appears not to have been addressed is how such individuals interact with each other. I have observed one surprising pattern, namely, a level of mutual support, mutual defence, and concurrence on positions, particularly when a member with an affinitive style is radically challenged. Given the self-centredness inherent in all these disorders, such alliances become quite intriguing regardless of how temporary they may be. One explanation, offered by Obeid (1999), suggests that by affirming each other as individuals they tend to affirm the viability of mendacity and manipulativeness in the face of ethical intimidation. Thus, this solidarity is a strategic counter-intimidation aimed against those who brandish the swords of truthfulness and honesty and expect speedy gains.

Personality Disorders and Political Organizations

One of the pivotal traits in personality disorders, and particularly of the flamboyant ones, is the proclivity to attack the *ego* of an adversary. The activities of impressing, charming, outwitting, outmanoeuvring, manipulating, competing with, undermining, and defeating are energies that are essentially directed at someone's ego instead of at an objective social task that is intrinsically viable. Even when these individuals undertake organized projects within a political party, their ultimate motive is either self-aggrandizement or the outbidding and challenging of someone. Their self-expression and self-affirmation are drastically dependent on the presence of other egos in a convenient setting, one where they can "feed" on the attention and the polemics generated. Accordingly, the psychological survival of these individuals is tied parasitically to the political movement which can provide them with their preferred mediums of self-expression. The sacrifice of ideological and other abstract commitment, demoralization, and loss of party cohesiveness are the inevitable outcomes of this *ego-centred* and *ego-targetting* approach.

People involved in political movements often attribute many expressions of unprincipled, corrupt, and traitorous behaviour to human nature or to the nature of political enterprise itself. These attributions are dangerously generalized and inaccurate. A closer examination will likely reveal that most of the divisive behaviour is perpetrated by or is a repercussion of the conduct of only a few entrenched individuals, often those with disordered personalities who tend be devious and corrupt, and for whom political strategy is synonymous with deceit. It is the disordered, the weak, and the inadequate personalities that corrupt politics. Wholesome personalities resist being corrupted by the political office or by corrupt colleagues, and the large number of political leaders who act with integrity testify to this.

It is my opinion that ideological political movements, particularly in developing countries, that seek the realization of social ideals will not go very far unless they develop mechanisms to limit the presence of camouflaged antisocials in their ranks. Pathological narcissism appears to be the disorder most implicated in the politics of developing countries. The founding members of any political movement will be destined to circuitous, bumpy, and thorny paths if they include within their ranks individuals with personality disorders. The ideals, the values, and the goals of an aspiring political movement will be drastically compromised if it fails to recognize the various personality cocktails of pathological narcissism, psychopathy, Machiavellianism, and paranoia that it is bound to attract as soon as it achieves a measure of success. Procedures for identification, screening-out, and the removal of disordered personalities should be promoted as essential managerial and leadership skills in any political movement with authentic social ideals.

Hare (1993) said of psychopaths that "If we cannot spot them, we are doomed to be their victims, both as individuals and as a society"; this also applies to all other personality disorders. A traditional managerial wisdom needs to be reclaimed in politics, namely, that if you want to have partners who are loyal, ethical, and with congenial personalities, you will have to recruit them, and that is not an easy task.

Can Camouflaged Aggression Become Addictive?

We have seen that personality disorders provide a motivational disposition for engaging in camouflaged aggression and can lend extremism and chronicity to it. The question arises whether camouflaged aggression can be further propelled by its own psychological momentum and adaptation; that is, can it become addictive?

In responding to this question, it should be emphasized that camouflaged aggression involves mental games, which if successfully performed, can alleviate boredom, boost a sense of power, and reduce alienation. Being psychologically rewarding, these mental games can become the medium of an obsessive-compulsive preoccupation among "normals." It is feasible that techniques of camouflaged aggression can become compulsive expressions, as in the case of impulse-ridden forms of neuroses observed in gambling and in certain forms of promiscuous sexual behaviour. Furthermore, techniques of camouflaged aggression, as described in Chapter 3, can be relied upon as means of power acquisition and, as a result of being intimately tied to power, they can be pursued for their own sake; they become, like power, goals in themselves. Although all the chronic dispensers of camouflaged aggression I have known also appeared to possess a broader form of character pathology, I have heard about "nice guys" who were chronically obsessed with manipulation and power games. One senior administrator is reported to have confessed, "If I cannot find someone to manipulate, I will manipulate myself." The addictive dimension of camouflaged aggression is an area that is often overlooked and requires further research.

The Impact of Camouflaged Aggression on Health

The research on physical and emotional stressors in the workplace and their impact on health is extensive. Two main characteristics of camouflaged aggression need to be noted in this context. First, camouflaged aggression has a slow cathartic release. The protracted nature of this aggression and its suppression of anger slows down the cathartic process and allows aggression to accumulate in individuals engaging in it. What further slows down the cathartic process is the structurally induced reliance on the displacement of aggression. Berkowitz, Cochrane, and Embree (1981) have contended that intensely frustrated individuals can reduce their aggression only through the infliction of harm upon the actual frustrater or aggressor. Successful catharsis appears to be tied not to any discharge of aggression but to successful attainment of the aggressive goal, namely, the retaliation against the actual perpetrator (if he or she can be identified). Unexpressed aggression can induce a host of psychosomatic illnesses.

Second, the masked nature of camouflaged aggression disorganizes the experience and the reaction to aggression. The difficulty in identifying the injury and in locating blame diffuses consciousness of conflict and precludes proper differentiation, proper channeling, and subsequent externalization of hostility. The lack of identification and channeling of aggression can lead to its denial: "there is no problem." Instead of "psychologizing" and externalizing conflict and aggression, denial leads to their somatization. The excessive reliance on the mechanism of denial was found to be associated with the development of cancer (see, e.g., Simonton, 1978). Thus, camouflaged aggression, by disorganizing the reaction to aggression, can lead certain individuals to deny their victimization and their need to retaliate, and accordingly induces them to redirect aggression against their bodies, increasing the risk of developing serious illnesses.

The Porcupine Entanglement

The prolonged interaction with a disordered personality—whether at the general interpersonal level or within the context of an organization— is often an unpleasant and distressing experience. Such experience can be analogically comparable to a thorny encounter with a porcupine. Similar distress can be experienced as a result of interacting with an organization that is poorly managed or comprises individuals with personality disorders. In both cases the victim regrets the involvement and yearns for a speedy exit, having learned the lesson of caution regarding such encounters. The *porcupine effect* has been used in psychological literature (see, e.g., Maner et al., 2007; Frank, 2017) to refer to behaviour that seeks to be more protective than usual, often in relation to intimacy and involvement. The anticipated need for caution and self-defence results from the recurrence of pain after interacting with a certain relationship or system.

Social complexity increases the need of individuals to seek the services of diverse public agencies. Most public agencies continuously exert managerial and administrative efforts to improve the quality and efficiency of services delivered. Attention to customer satisfaction and ethicality in behaviour is expected. However, many departments of public and private organizations are run by personnel who are diverse in education, experience, culture, and personality, and are managed (and mismanaged) within bureaucratic settings. Individuals applying to these agencies run a substantial risk of being misconstrued, ignored, delayed, misdirected, rudely treated, becoming fodder for the self-aggrandizement of officials. The involvement of several officials tends to compromise the client's privacy and create undue embarrassment for him or her. Attempts by the client to rectify things may add to the confusion, conflict, and waste of time, with the client wishing he never sought assistance or applied. The interaction with such agencies may result not only in frustration, agony, and loss of time, but also in humiliation. The presence of personnel with the previously described personality disorders (e.g., narcissists, passive-aggressives, and histrionics) increases the likelihood of this outcome. Also, agencies that are located in countries that tolerate administrative corruption further aggravate the distress. Accordingly, a porcupine effect needs to be cultivated with respect to such agencies and associations owing to the anticipation of a thorny entanglement akin to an entanglement with a porcupine.

The above experience resembles that of the previously described ego bashing but is delivered by more than one incumbent within the bureaucratic entity. This experience also expands on Nietzsche's concept of the "economy of the self." Nietzsche (1882/1968) recommended that an intellectually mature individual should conserve his or her self-energy by refraining from overreacting to unimportant issues and avoiding involvement with trivial people and their trivial issues. Accordingly, a second recommendation is made here regarding the economy of self and dignity: Avoid entanglement with agencies where you suspect character disorders or poor management. Avoidance and distance need to be maintained in relation to certain organizations that exhibit the traits of lurking porcupines.

Diagnosing Personality Disorders by Means of a Balance Sheet

An important relationship that may be worth investigating is the ratio between the positive and the negative input that an organization receives from an employee with a personality disorder. Despite their destructive potential, persons with personality disorders have been observed to embark on certain organizational tasks with great zeal and efficiency, sometimes "beyond the call of duty." Their zeal, which is often short-lived, can produce spectacular results. Their strikingly positive input can neutralize a great deal of their past negative input, but it can be seen as part of a manipulative strategy, an attempt to smoke screen an ugly record. I am tempted, on the basis of my observations, to go a step further. I would hypothesize the existence of a deeply embedded formula that ensures that the negative input of the disordered person will ultimately outweigh the positive input. This ratio is somehow mathematically programmed at an unconscious level and is destined to be tilted against the organization.

This ratio could be investigated through the development of a longitudinal investigation that would record the inputs of such subjects and assess them by means of a negative/positive weighted scale. If the results tilt in favour of negative organizational input, then this relationship can also be used for the diagnostic identification of personality disorders within organizations. This balance sheet assessment could be an alternative to the diagnosis on the basis of clinical observation.

SOCIOCULTURAL FACTORS
IN CAMOUFLAGED AGGRESSION

THE NATURE OF AND INTERACTION between individual personalities and organizational structures make all of us susceptible to become perpetrators, and victims, of camouflaged aggression. In addition to the situational and personality factors, there are sociocultural factors that contribute to its propagation.

Alienation

Contemporary Western society encourages people to strive for individualized goals, self-actualization, and success, usually in the form of financial independence and consumerism. However, professional success and access to consumer goods may not lead to the acquisition of actual power and autonomy since true power positions in society are few and difficult to attain. Furthermore, a culture that emphasizes individualism hinders the development of cohesive social groups, ones that can offer their members a sense of belonging and identity. Thus, many people, particularly in large urban societies, experience social alienation, the symptoms of which are a sense of isolation, powerlessness, and meaninglessness. Some individuals react to their sense of alienation by engaging in camouflaged aggression; they engage in the power games associated with camouflaged aggression in order to compensate for feelings of powerlessness and marginality.

Anomie

"Anomie" is a term coined by Durkheim (1897/1951) over one hundred years ago to refer to the state of normative disorganization resulting from rapid social change; it is often associated with high rates of suicide. Subsequent studies (e.g., Sellin, 1938) found the anomie resulting from migration, mobility, cultural heterogeneity, and cultural conflict to be associated with the presence of crime and addiction. For Durkheim social norms have two main functions: a) regulation of behaviour by prescribing what to do and what to expect, and b) control of behaviour by prescribing what not to do. Norms also regulate and control psychosocial drives such as ambition, quest for money, and social power. These drives have an infectious quality and are not easily contained; they require stable norms to control them. When the commitment to uniform norms is undermined, their regulative and controlling function weakens, and this in turn leads to uncertainty, social and political apathy, lack of endorsement of belief systems, and increased rates of suicide and crime. Because they lack strong attachments to socially accepted norms, individuals experiencing anomia (anomie at the individual, subjective level) are less likely to resist indulging in camouflaged aggression. They are also less likely to restrain others from employing it.

Malignant aggression within the organization is particularly aggravated by the presence of anomie. Malignant aggression was defined in Chapter 3 as aggression that is stripped of its normative function; it is aggression driven by the need for tension release and by situational convenience (I am hurting you because I can and because it makes me feel better). Such regressive expression of aggression within the organization, as was earlier suggested, is similar to that of random mass murder. Both have anomie as an underlying etiological factor.

For example, after being subjected to a lengthy period of camouflaged aggression, an employee might return to his workplace with a gun and shoot not at an identified culprit, but at anyone he encounters. The aggressive action is unfocused, blind, and nihilistic.

The violent perpetrator is often construed as suffering from personality abnormalities or psychopathology; investigations advanced by the media tend to dwell on biographical factors in the offender's personal history. These factors, which are common to millions of non-criminal others, in fact explain little; meanwhile, little attention is paid to the socially structured camouflaged aggression as part of the problem.

Learning and Cultural Transmission

The acquisition and dissemination of camouflaged aggression within and between social groups, and through them to the culture as a whole, is a simple learning process. Interaction in an organization in which camouflaged aggression is prevalent (i.e., most organizations) leads to a type of learning that takes place in close association with others (Sutherland, 1947). It consists of two processes: the first is the learning of techniques or behavioural skills, and the second is the learning of attitudes and rationalizations that justify and legitimate such behaviour.

Social learning theory emphasizes the interactive nature of cognitive, behavioural, and environmental determinants. According to Albert Bandura (1986), the leading scholar of the social learning approach, this learning takes place in two steps: First, the person observes how others act and then acquires a mental picture of the act and its consequences. Second, the person acts out the acquired image, and if the consequences are positive, he or she tends to repeat the action. The learning process is enhanced when the emulated models possess authority and charisma.

Camouflaged aggression is transmitted (both as a technique and as a normatively accepted practice) from one generation of employees to the next by means of those learning processes. Its acquisition through learning processes helps to explain the different levels of camouflaged aggression within similar sections of an organization. High levels of entrenchment of camouflaged aggression in certain sections is often traceable to particular individuals who initiated its practice.

Narcissistic Values

In *The Culture of Narcissism*, Christopher Lasch (1979) proposed that the personality features found in pathological narcissism are becoming the characteristics of the norms and social orientations of large segments of contemporary North American society. Self-centredness, self-aggrandizement, entitlement, and manipulativeness are promoted and reinforced by contemporary economic and social trends. Individualism, which involves a lack of connectedness to a cohesive group and an emphasis on personal success and material gain, has led pathological personality characteristics to become viewed not only as acceptable but as admirable.

The impact of the narcissistic normative style on camouflaged aggression is apparent and significant. The more managers become geared toward self-aggrandizement in terms of personal power and financial gain, the more they are motivated to use the organization for their personal ends, the more antagonism they are likely to draw from others, and the more likely they are to resort to manipulation and deception in order to realize their goals.

It was pointed out earlier that the classic bureaucrat is committed to the status quo and resists innovative and creative ideas. But it is important to add in this context that serious threat to creative ideas is frequently perpetrated by the narcissistic administrator. New ideas are not suppressed because they constitute a challenge to the status quo, but because they are an affront to the narcissism of the department head. The new idea is suppressed not because it lacks merit but because it was proposed by someone else: the administrator's name would not appear in the final report or in the published paper; nor would he or she be delivering a talk on the research idea in a conference attended by peers. In other words, glory goes to someone else. Suppressing or sabotaging a new idea or project cannot be done by flat rejection; rather, it is managed by subterfuges, typically orchestrated with an initial theoretical endorsement of the idea and a subsequent bemoaning of administrative roadblocks or lack of funding.

Cross-Cultural Values and Importation

Culture can substantially influence the way conflicts are interpreted and reacted to. Cultural values and norms can help one to understand some of the dynamics of workplace aggression; they can also be employed to moderate and control aggression. Studies on cross-cultural differences in workplace aggression have dealt with the various topics such as the impact of perceptions of power, formality, collectivity, civility, and supervision (see, e.g., Li & Lim, 2017).

Interactions in organizations that I have observed in an Arabian Gulf country indicate that camouflaged aggression in its Western expression is not yet entrenched in the bureaucracies of these countries. However, other forms of interpersonal conflicts, such as status rivalries and group alliances, appear to be prevalent. The relatively small size of these organizations and the lesser reliance on formalization in upper management (where disputes are resolved face-to-face) may be partially responsible for the apparently low incidence of camouflaged aggression. But three culturally ingrained factors appear to have a significant impact in containing camouflaged aggression: 1) values of honour and masculinity; 2) the related Arab cultural tendency to openly express conflicts (position taking, value declaration, hostility, blame, rationalization) among coworkers; and 3) the tendency to engage others in the dispute in order to solicit their input for the ultimate goal of conflict resolution.

First, the value of honour, as suggested before, is essentially abstract. Abstraction inevitably leads to demarcation of conflict and to its conscious confrontation. The recipients of camouflaged aggression respond to the aggression not as part of an organizational strategy or game but as a breach of a more abstract cultural value; they see it, for instance, as a betrayal of friendship, a "stab in the back," or "treachery." Such a highly negative perception of camouflaged aggression strengthens the reaction against it. Masculine values that endorse honour, and open challenge, are also confrontational. The second factor, the cultural tendency that seeks open expression of disagreements and declaration of positions, is also confrontational. By verbalizing the dispute openly to others, the strategic orientation toward the conflict necessarily becomes that of reconciliation. The third factor, the culturally ingrained tendency to involve others in the dispute and to seek their judgment and intervention, further moves the conflict away from camouflage. This typically Arab tendency to involve others in a private dispute is also related to abstraction. The interpersonal conflict becomes transformed into an issue, and, as such, takes on a universal quality. Universality implies commonality in that the conflict is found and recurs in all similar settings. Accordingly, the conflict is not unique and could be shared with others. Thus, abstraction encourages disclosure while concreteness encourages privacy and non-disclosure (Abdennur, 2014, Chapter 3).

This type of issue expression was displayed, as I recall, through a symbolic gesture performed by one of my hosts, a senior director. He placed a bottle of tranquillizers on his desk in full view in an attempt to highlight the fact that his current dispute with another director was causing him a great deal of stress. Hostile remarks, criticisms, and justifications from both parties involved other concerned staff in the dispute, who in turn exerted efforts toward a reconciliation. Camouflaged aggression presupposes the exact opposite strategy; it demands suppression and masking of hostility through smiles and denials, despite mobilization for a protracted, insidious, and undeclared war. This confrontational cultural orientation, if encouraged and refined, can delay or block the spread of this organizational virus in countries that have not yet been plagued by it.

There is another dimension to social learning and cultural transmission; it is the *importation* of camouflaged aggression into cultures where such techniques have heretofore been absent. This importation can be observed to take place when, after acquiring educational and organization experience in a developed country, an individual from a less developed society returns home and takes over an administrative position. Many returning graduates and professionals bring back to their countries more than professional knowledge and expertise. Techniques of camouflaged aggression may well be part of the returner's luggage and items that are secretly prized as tools of a "superior intellect." These techniques become superimposed on entrenched, problematic behaviours, such as influence peddling, and can aggravate the current organizational failures in such societies. Imported camouflaged aggression often takes hold among those who have secure positions, light workloads, and no inclination to pursue productive or creative work. Camouflaged aggression can thus become the preferred sport of the idle and the uncreative employee in developing countries.

Anti-Confrontation Values

The fourth major contributory factor is normative and ideological in nature; it is represented by all of the unexamined notions, misconceptions, clichés, and faulty inferences that are employed to implicitly define confrontational action as dangerous and uncivilized. This ideological repertoire does not represent an intellectually integrated position toward aggression; rather, it is more of a chain of value assumptions and inferences that, in a concerted way, serves to promote negative attitudes toward confrontation. I have identified eight such notions.

1. Violence as Absolutely Bad

Since the 1980s, the public understanding of the term "violence" has been undergoing a metamorphosis. The preoccupation with violence in the sensationalized context of spousal and sexual assault has led to the overloading of the meaning of the word. The preoccupation with such forms of assault has extended understandings of the term beyond its traditional dictionary definition, such as the use of physical force to injure or to abuse, and to refer to many behaviours that are aggressive or destructive but not necessarily violent in the original sense of the word. This conceptual overloading reached its peak during the 1980s and 1990s, but has now receded due to the influence of organized research. Most calls for zero tolerance for workplace violence during that period included verbal and emotional abuse as expressions of violence. This overloading of the concept of violence has led to a widespread downplaying of the seriousness of non-violent forms of aggression, forms which can be more injurious but go unrecognized. For example, punching someone will elicit far greater expression of outrage than permanently victimizing someone by behaving in ways which lead them to a nervous breakdown.

The term "violence" has also undergone another transformation. In popular media (particularly during the 1980s and 1990s) the term became synonymous with "vice," a term which connotes wickedness or evil. Violent behaviour used to be viewed as behaviour that is physically injurious and that, though regrettable, might at times be necessary as in self-protection or in defence of dignity and freedom. But attempts were made to present violent aggression as inherently pathological, evil, and taboo. This shift was likely intended to a weaken the taboos traditionally placed on deviant forms of sexual behaviour which do not involve violence. For example, virtually all forms of sexual activity previously associated with "vice," "immorality," or "perversion" are now considered to be acceptable as long as they do not involve physical acts of aggression or children. We are urged to think that any resort to violence is unthinkable. This trend has culminated in the attempt to legislate zero tolerance for violence over the past two decades in some North American jurisdictions. This zero tolerance crusade focused on workplace violence, domestic violence, and sexual violence against women. The interventions for achieving this goal rely basically on common methods used to deal with other types of crime. A question arises: Why not advocate zero tolerance for all crime? The targetting of violence in these particular domains was an unsuccessful attempt to deploy absolute thinking and taboos for political purposes, an endeavour that is doomed to clash with social science disciplined thinking.

The expression of aggression can be influenced by modal preferences pertaining to masculinity and femininity. For example, male serial killers often shoot or bludgeon their victims. Female serial killers are more likely to poison their victims, but males and females are equally prone to stabbing. Men more often rob while women defraud. Gender may continue to influence modal orientations.

The sensationalized linking of violent aggression to terrorism and the preoccupation with control of firearms serves to promote the false message that violent forms of behaviour are the only danger and serves to distract attention away from other serious threats to society (e.g., hedonism), and from the fact that the violent forms of aggression may be a response to camouflaged forms.

Placing absolute taboos on a biosocial drive largely representing the confrontational mode tilts the modal balance of aggression in favour of non-confrontational methods and paves the way for camouflage and institutional domination.

2. Confrontation Is a Manifestation of Violence

When interpersonal violent aggression is presented as though it were the only form of injurious behaviour, and as an irrational, uncivilized, and unthinkable option, confrontation, which is often a concomitant of violent aggression, comes to be viewed in the same way. Thus, the term "confrontation" becomes equated with belligerence, intransigence, danger, and irrationality. This ideology extols the virtues of compromise, negotiation, tolerance, pragmatism, and an unconditional commitment to conflict resolution. The virtues that may be associated with a confrontational strategy, such as the speedy identification of a problem, the emergence of explicit moral positions, and the confinement of conflict to the parties concerned, are downplayed or ignored.

The attitudes and notions that are depreciative of confrontation tend to be items in the ideological repertoire of individuals who evidence the *conflict avoidant* personality syndrome (Abdennur, 1987; see also Chapter 4 of this book). That such a personality style has become idealized is symptomatic of the fact that unconditional compromise and avoidance of conflict have achieved institutional dominance in Western countries.

The difference between passive aggression and camouflaged aggression was described in detail in Chapter 1. Passive-aggressive behaviour takes place predominantly within interpersonal relations. Camouflaged aggression, according to the bimodal theory, requires organizational structures for its delivery and masking. But the structures of complex systems are invading all interpersonal and social relationships; society is indeed being formalized as Parsons (1951) predicted. Thus, the increase of structural opportunities to aggress passively at the interpersonal level will increase both the incidence of passive-aggression and the fixations on this expression (the passive-aggressive personality disorder).

Despite the ties of this personality disorder to the increasing organizational and interpersonal complexity, it was dropped from the list of personality disorders in the fourth (1994) and fifth (2013) editions of the American Psychiatric Association's *Diagnostic and Statistical Manual of Mental Disorders*. The question that arises is whether the elimination of the passive-aggressive disorder represents a recent normative acceptance of this form of behaviour. Has the practice of presenting a placid and civilized front while vehemently attempting to harm another become the rule rather than the exception?

3. Direct Retaliation Is Revenge

One of the tenets of the anti-confrontation ideology is its repudiation of direct retaliatory action, which is depreciatively labelled as "revenge." However, retaliating in an explicit, direct, and personal manner against an individual who has injured you can have many redeeming social benefits, some of them already mentioned in this text. The most important organizational benefits of confrontative retaliation are that 1) it brings the conflict into the open, 2) it speeds up conflict resolution, 3) it confines aggression to the two parties involved, thus preventing its displacement throughout the organization, 4) it promotes deterrence, and 5) it makes a moral statement. When the injury involves behaviour that violates a principle or an ethical code, then open retaliation enables vindication of that principle.

Retributive vengeance may be regarded as morally inferior to the Christian response of "turning the other cheek," a reaction that attempts to substitute love for anger. However, such a response is rare in an organization, and most of those who repudiate open revenge do not "turn the other cheek," but instead look to see if they can find a way to exact revenge. Empirical evidence reviewed by Bies, Tripp, and Kramer (1997) supports a functional view of revenge in organizations. In cases where the victim retaliated directly against the aggressor, revenge tended to have constructive and prosocial effects. Private confrontations tended to be followed by reconciliation and explicit acts of revenge tended to deter the aggressor from doing further harm.

Research by Jones (2013) indicated that harm on its own is not the main motivator in revenge. Revenge is motivated by the belief that the offender's actions are both intentional (malevolent) and morally repugnant.

Abstraction is also an important factor in determining the duration of revenge feelings and the severity of retaliation. When transgressions are viewed not as mere slights or foresights but as violations of abstract principles pertaining to ethics, friendship, or family loyalty, they become difficult to forget or forgive. I have analyzed in more detail (Abdennur, 2014) how feelings of allegiance, memory of past events, gratitude for good deeds, and revenge for insults can be augmented and persevered in memory as a result of abstraction. Honour and dignity are in fact abstract constructions of self, ones that explain the enduring memory and severe reactions to insults suffered by those who uphold these values. Feelings and acts of revenge may also be a result of pathological narcissism, perhaps owing to perceived injuries to the aggrandized self-image of the narcissist. It is more common today for revenge to take place as a result of a slighted narcissistic self-image than a slighted sense of honour.

It is important to stress the distinction between direct retaliatory or *confrontational* revenge and *getting even* revenge. Confrontational revenge should be viewed as an important and informal social control mechanism, one which can orient the revenge reaction toward more formal and legalistic control procedures. On the other hand, the getting even revenge is a destructive approach that deserves our moral contempt. The normative acceptance of the latter strategy is highly ingrained in contemporary organizational culture and guided by the slogan "don't get angry, get even." The "getting even" approach is often one that avoids direct confrontation with the aggressor. It is a more protracted process that involves organizational structures, a great deal of waiting and stalking, and the eventual delivery of aggression in a camouflaged form.

4. Forgiveness as the Ideal Alternative

When retaliation or efforts to achieve reconciliation are abandoned, forgiveness may surface as the preferred alternative. From certain religious or spiritual perspectives, it is considered as the sublime or ideal strategy. But given the law of conservation of energy and the hydraulic principle of aggression, we cannot always expect a happy outcome from forgiveness. Displacement is inevitable, or as Nietzsche puts it, "It is impossible to suffer without making someone pay for it" (1886/1967, p. 44).

If we search carefully for the displacements resulting from blockage of revenge in forgiveness, we may find them in remote and masked states such as endorsements of values that undermine social effectiveness. Values of extreme tolerance and liberalized acceptance compromise radical solutions to social problems. These values, ones that are frequently endorsed by the forgivers, can be seen as displaced vengeance taken against society as a whole. In short, free-floating love can be more dangerous than free-floating hostility.

5. Deceit Is Smart

Behind the increasing acceptance of non-confrontation is the tendency to equate deception and manipulation with intelligence, mental superiority, or shrewdness. This notion is reinforced by the perception of the victim of deception as stupid. Deceit and artifice have come to be seen as necessary skills for achieving and holding public office, or for a successful legal career, and are considered essential for statesmanship. This mindset in a bureaucrat can become dangerous as it encourages the spread of manipulativeness within the organization. The equating of deceit with intelligence tends to flatter the narcissism of the perpetrator as it is linked to the characteristics of successful and great individuals. As the growing endorsement of manipulativeness spreads to society at large, citizens come to believe that they must acquire skill in interpersonal manipulation in order to not feel at risk of being victimized or to appear stupid by those who are more "socially skilled."

Deception and manipulation have become valued, and even essential, interpersonal skills. But they are skills that do not belong to the domain of higher intellectual and scientific thinking, and are likely to be inversely correlated with genuine and creative accomplishments in the sciences. The rudimentary forms of deceit, such as those of false representation, are common among most living species, as noted by Rue (1994) in the following example. The courtship behaviour of the male hanging fly involves bringing a gift of food to the female, which she eats as the male copulates with her. Some males of the species dupe other males by mimicking female courtship behaviour. When the gift-bearing male arrives, the impersonator snatches the food away and eats it.

According to Rue (1994), the important question, from an evolutionary perspective, is not how camouflage and mimicry resemble lying and pretending in humans, but how human lying and pretending represent instances of camouflage and mimicry found in most living species. He suggests that it is time we quit thinking of deception as a characteristic exclusive to human interactions.

The mastery of rudimentary forms of interpersonal deception by individuals with a low level of intelligence testifies to the instinctual basis of deceit. The ingenuity of the psychopath's deceitfulness appears to be related to his or her ability for spontaneous tuning to the instinctual bases of deception. Higher education and training in scientific fields tend to thwart the freedom from objectivity that is required for effective deceit. Disciplined scientists who are versed in scientific research tend to lose the ability for deception. Freud complained that his rigorous analytic interests in psychological phenomena rendered him unable to lie (1938/1964). In short, anyone may employ deception, but the long-term success of an organizational career or position cannot depend on manipulation.

Objective analysis and confrontation must replace manipulation and deception within public organizations. Conniving needs to be replaced by convincing. Convincing is an intellectual skill which can result in sustainable change in others' attitudes, whereas conniving can only yield brief success, often followed by the eventual detection and subsequent hostility of the victim. Managers who are capable of being objective, analytical, and forthright have no need for manipulation.

6. Pseudo-Confrontation

The essential characteristics of the confrontational position are an objective and comprehensive awareness of an issue and direct communication with the responsible party. There are many ways an attitude or an issue can be expressed. The context and cultural norms tend to shape the style of expression, but confrontation is not merely a *style* of delivery; it is one of the two *modes* that are the central strategies in the expression and communication of aggression. The mode of delivery is what most significantly qualifies the action and the response to it. Not all outward and flamboyant expression qualifies as confrontational expression. For example, interpersonal directness, belligerent assertiveness, rudeness, and argumentativeness can be used to avoid focusing on and dealing with the central issue. This pseudo-confrontational

approach can give the impression of frankness and straightforward-
ness ("calling a spade a spade") while in reality it expresses an avoidance
strategy in the guise of confrontation. Exhibitionistic statements that
explicitly describe private affairs or divulge personal information can
also be used to give the impression of the speaker's frankness and objectivity. It is thus possible to confront the person without confronting the
issue, or to confront the person in order to avoid the issue.

Assertion and confrontation are not the same thing. Assertiveness as
taught in innumerable social skills training courses (e.g., see Lange &
Jakubowski, 1978) focuses on the clear, direct, and open expression of
feelings, attitudes, and points of views by an individual in interpersonal
situations. But because the focus is on learning to identify and express
feelings and perspectives (albeit with respect for those of others), assertiveness is often only self-serving. It may help a person to relate better to
people but may cause him or her to lose sight of the issue at hand, and
to fail to take into consideration broader principles or values.

Assertive communication, in the sense of expressing a clear statement of one's feelings and position on an issue, may boost confrontation
through enhancing clarity. However, adequate confrontation requires
more than a mere open expression of one's feelings and views. A shy or
a modest expressive style can be highly confrontational if the individual
zeros in on the issue and directs it to the right party. Assertiveness is
neither necessary nor sufficient for confrontation.

7. The Neutralization of Conflict by Means of Institutionalized Hypocrisy

A conflict between two individuals has two central components: a) the
existence of two opposed sets of intentions or views, and b) the conscious
and affective expression of this opposition. Organizations, by means of
structural and normative operations, can make possible the isolation of
these two components so that the aggressive aspect of conflict is
expressed independently of its affective manifestations. For example,
two employees may be actively engaged in camouflaged aggression
against each other and, at the same time, manage to carry out a placid

and cordial interaction, one that suppresses or neutralizes the experience and outward expression of opposition and hostility. Behind the
scenes, the two protagonists may in fact be engaged in elaborate plots
and intrigues to undermine and block each other. However, at the
surface interpersonal level, they may salute, smile, and join the group
for coffee, cracking jokes and sharing anecdotes.

This display of polite behaviour is not only hypocritical but manages
to neutralize the manifest affective components of conflict. Acts that
are intended to harm are isolated from their affective and moral
components, depriving the organization from the benefits of a full and
conscious (dialectical) experiencing of conflict and resolution.

When a power differential exists between two such employees, a new
dynamic may surface. The stronger party can use politesse to neutralize
the weaker party's retaliatory reactions without having to reduce the
degree of harming. This relationship in fact amounts to psychological
disarming. In this disarmed state the weaker party endures suffering
from two sources: a) from the perpetuation of the injurious actions, and
b) from the frustration of the need to openly retaliate, thus resulting in a
redirection of anger toward the self.

8. The Non-Confrontational Values of the "Minimal Self"

The concept of the "minimal self" was proposed by Christopher Lasch
(1984) to describe a constricted experiencing of the self (as a converse of
the grand and expansive narcissistic thrust) and the pursuit of survival
as an end in itself. Survival in modern society is often valued uncondi-
tionally without any regard to quality of life. Notions that promote the
extending of life through medical technology regardless of the quality of
life, pronouncements such as "I am just trying to survive" or "I am just
trying to earn a living" are examples of evaluations that point to survival
as the ultimate purpose. The contemporary attitude that "nothing is
worth dying for" in effect means that "nothing is worth living for." The
quest for world peace has taken on added urgency since the coming of
the nuclear age; however, as stated by Feher and Heller (1982; quoted

by Lasch, 1984), "there is still a contradiction between a good life and a mere life...violence and wars cannot be entirely eliminated from our actions if we seek something more than survival" (p. 74). The Darwinian notion of survival as the driving force and ultimate purpose of life is not only minimalist, it is also regressive since it undermines the active role humans have in challenging and transforming their social environment and in deciding what kind of life is worth living.

An expression of the minimal experiencing of the self is paranoid thinking. This thinking arises from deep-seated feelings of powerlessness that minimize confrontative strategies and restrict them to the service of defence or counteraction. Another expression of this minimal state of self can be observed in the popular rush to be seen as a victim. The social and political rhetoric that extol the moral superiority of "victims" tends to mask the aggressive, vindictive, greedy, and ambitious aims of many of the "victimized."

The values of the minimal self can be better depicted by contrasting them with the traditional confrontative values emanating from an expansive, principled, and resolute self. The following story told by the celebrated Lebanese folk writer Salam Rassy (1976) illustrates the traditional contrasting values. During the early 1960s, Rassy went to the mountainous village of Shibaa in the south of Lebanon to look for an individual whom he had previously hired to do some work. Finding the worker's house, he knocked on the door.

A young man opened and reciprocated my greeting. I asked him whether the man I was looking for was in. He replied, "What do you want from him?" Then the voice of an old man thundered from inside the house: "Mahmoud: if you know where your brother is, say where he is...we are not in the habit of hiding our men." He went on to say, "You cannot hide a javelin in a sack." (p. 76)

The image of hiding a javelin or a spear in a sack is both graphic and symbolic. A javelin is usually too long to be covered by a sack. Even if it can be covered, the javelin will pierce the sack thus making its concealment difficult. But most contemporary bureaucrats can easily be hidden in organizational sacks; they are conveniently curved and lacking in any piercing or thrusting capacity. Individuals who walk tall, those who have views and can express them directly and without resorting to a victim role, are becoming a rare breed. In contrast, conflict avoiders, survivalists, and various kinds of minimalists, those who can be easily deployed, easily displayed, and easily hidden, are dominating the cultural scene.

6

PREVENTION AND CONTROL
OF CAMOUFLAGED AGGRESSION

AN UNDERLYING ASSUMPTION of the theory presented in
this book is that a need to express aggression is an inevitable
consequence of the conflicts that occur in all human interactions. Aggression is an intricate and crucial part of the
biological and social evolution of the human species.
Aggression is not inherently bad: it can be either instrumen-
tally useful and socially functional or harmful and
dysfunctional, depending on the goals it is intended to serve.
Excessive aggression, if prolonged, can be disruptive of social
activity and accordingly it needs to be managed and controlled,
but not suppressed, denied, or tabooed.

The challenge of reducing aggression requires two strategies:

1. Reducing its fundamental causes such as deprivation,
   injustice, overcrowding, stress, and disorganization.
2. Managing its expression in ways which minimize its
   excesses and the damage it can cause and which maximize the personal and social benefits it can yield.

Neither of those goals can be achieved by approaches that
are limited to the control and suppression of confrontational
aggression. Their achievement also requires the management

of camouflaged aggression since its unchecked expression increases the quantum of aggression that is generated and warehoused in organizations.

There is a recent upsurge of research on workplace aggression, much of it focusing on intervention. According to Leiter, Peck, and Baccardax (2017), much is known about the triggers and outcomes of workplace aggression but little is known about intervention approaches and their efficacy. The authors survey the current intervention strategies, which include policy initiatives, legislation, training programs, and team-based actions. These interventions have been largely based on intuitive and logical judgment; few empirical assessments have been undertaken. The authors think that scientific research on interventions for workplace aggression is in its infancy. They also suggest that different intervention approaches reflect distinct perspectives on the nature of aggression; however, all interventions need to be guided by a basic strategy that stresses: 1) the importance of awareness of the problem, 2) identifying the behaviour as harmful, 3) assignment of accountability, 4) describing resolutions to victims, and 5) disclosing the administration's position and response.

The "organizational and managerial wisdom" framework (Kessler & Bailey, 2007) places recommendations such as those described above under the umbrella concept of wisdom. Organizational and managerial wisdom is seen as the ability to use one's intelligence, creativity, and knowledge, as mediated by personal values, to arrive at judgments that serve the common good. Knowledge includes social science theory, experience that has been reflected upon, and understanding of cultural values and norms. Possessing vast analytic intelligence and practical knowledge may not be enough; a manager must also know how to apply it. Sternberg's (2005) defined managerial wisdom as a skill of balancing. The skilful balancing of the interests of the multiple constituents of the organization, and their intrapersonal, interpersonal, and extrapersonal relationships, is necessary to achieve healthy adaptations and modifications. The wisdom and necessary skills, according to Jordan and Sternberg (2007), can be developed through graduate business programs and job-related experience. This educational strategy involves understanding multiple points of view, contextualizing decisions in time and place, role modelling, and balancing all for the common good.

The recommended cognitive approach of this text can be seen as part of the wisdom framework. The cognitive approach focuses on the operations of thinking. Proper thinking essentially involves abstracting and moving beyond immediate, particular, or concrete conditions, seeing them as parts of a wider or general behaviour or context. Abstraction thus opens the way for considering multiple dimensions and, subsequently, for their integration with the assistance of theory. The abstract integrated perspective moves toward a balanced judgment in relation to the specific concern. Thus, the cognitive approach initiates and energizes the process of developing organizational wisdom, which integrates academic knowledge, cultural knowledge, and experience. This skill can be imparted via educational means as those recommended by Jordan and Sternberg (2007).

For the purposes of this chapter, balancing that is acquired from the cultivation of abstract thinking and wisdom is confined to that of balancing the two modes of aggression. In the Introduction, I argued that rigorous scientific research on workplace aggression may not be very useful. What a manager needs are basic knowledge in social science theories, awareness of the manifestations of aggression, and good judgment. This book, by presenting an overarching theoretical model and by identifying certain concepts, constructs, and relationships, contributes to a basic cognitive approach to organizational aggression.

Balancing the Two Modes

The central position taken in this text is that in a stable society and in a stable organization, aggression is self-containing and self-minimizing when avenues and dispositions for the expression of the two modes (camouflaged and confrontational) are available. When the expression of aggression is unevenly confined to one mode, then the imbalance will likely lead to increased spread and increased accumulation of aggression. The strategy of balance implies that both modes are integral parts of the expression of aggression within organizational behaviour. In complex systems, a level of camouflaged aggression is inevitable and can at times be functional. For example, a repeated encroachment by an employee on another's domain can be brought to a halt by having the victim activate all kinds of formal procedures in a camouflaged manner against the perpetrator. The prospect of being entangled in legalistic, complex, time-consuming, or expensive procedures can serve as a deterrent for blunt aggressive behaviour. However, many, or perhaps most, modern organizations seek only to control confrontation; meanwhile, camouflaged aggression remains unchecked. Intervention must seek to rectify the imbalance. What is presently required is not only a reduction in camouflaged aggression but also an increase in confrontation.

Intervention needs to take place at two main levels:

1. *Conceptual.* Recognition by management of the phenomenon of camouflaged aggression, its prevalence and its effects; analysis of the organization's approaches to the management of conflict; and critical questioning of explicit and implicit values and notions held by the organization vis-à-vis the expression of aggression.
2. *Practical.* Adoption by management of an explicit value position vis-à-vis expression of aggression; implementation of new policies and practices to support the value position; and re-education throughout the organization.

Balancing the Two Modes at the Conceptual Level

Rather than proposing some administrative changes or forms of sanctions or rewards, as might be used in a human engineering or behavioural approach to social control, I am recommending the above described *cognitive* approach. As discussed before, this cognitive approach stresses the abstract understanding of a problematic condition as distinguished from segmented, practical or hands-on understanding.

Abstract understanding basically relies on cognitive strategies with the following attributes: a) comprehensiveness, which means looking at the problematic behaviour in its larger context, i.e., how it is expressed in, and how it relates to, other settings; and b) the reliance on theory. A theory simplifies causal relationships, facilitating the understanding and prediction of particular incidents. A theory "travels light"; it is freed from the need of carrying information about specific conditions and incidents; to quote Kurt Lewin: "There is nothing as practical as a good theory" (1952, p. 169). Similarly, an adequate construct captures, universalizes, and simplifies clusters of behaviours.

Managers must make clear to employees the potentially destructive and regressive consequences of camouflaged aggression. However, before doing so, managers must acknowledge that they can be perpetrators of the behaviour themselves. They must learn to identify camouflaged aggression in all its manifestations and to recognize its potential for damage both to the organization and to the individuals in that organization.

Managers must then actively and explicitly debunk notions (their own and others) that contribute to the positive sanctioning of camouflaged aggression. The notions that need to be challenged are those that either explicitly or implicitly label the confrontation as negative (as discussed in Chapter 5). Managers must communicate the position that confrontation as a basic strategy is inherently healthy despite the existence of unhealthy direct expressions of aggression such as physical intimidation, yelling matches, argumentation, and open incivility. The strategy of camouflage may be instrumental in achieving certain goals and for a limited time, or for containing excessive expressions of direct aggression; however, it is inherently problematic and unhealthy, as can be inferred from the descriptions in Chapter 3. Techniques of confrontation vary with the organizational context and are directly revealed to the incumbent. Practical training is seldom needed; having confrontation-promoting values, sentiments, and cognitions may suffice. The latter would include the debunking of notions that equate manipulation with high-order intelligence, or those that equate confrontation with belligerence.

It is important that the intervention strategy seek to cultivate and appeal to the sense of *self-respect and honour* of each of the members of the organization. A sense of honour can be the most effective policing agency; its abstract status fosters an internal and external consistency. Management must promote the belief that deceit, manipulation, and treachery are not honourable. Then individuals will more likely act with restraint when faced with the option of behaving in ways that they consider demeaning or beneath their self-worth. A constriction in a sense of honour results when employees are treated as, or come to see themselves as, minimal entities concerned only with survival. The survivalist perspective undermines self-worth and inner self-direction, thus allowing the pro-organizational behaviour of employees to become contingent only on external factors.

Well-guided cognitive strategies for achieving effective management of aggression in organizations are those that adhere to the following basic tenet:

Confrontation IS the Ideal Strategy

Managers or trainers must exalt the benefits of confrontation, properly conceptualized within its broader social expression, that is, as comprehensive and critical consciousness, as transcendence over forms of evasion and camouflage, and as the strategy largely responsible for higher cultural evolution. Thus, I recommend the following alternative definition of confrontation:

1. *Objectivity.* It is the most fundamental tenet of confrontation; it is also the most essential condition for justice. Without an objective understanding of the aspects of a problematic condition, no just resolution can be achieved. Also, disciplined objectivity promotes a quest for truthfulness and discourages lying and deception. Conflicting parties need to objectively identify all the dimensions

of the concern, and this includes the identification of undeclared *interests,* personal *preferences,* implicit *value assumptions,* the *benefits,* and *philosophical implications* of the problematic behaviour.

2. *Abstraction and Comprehensiveness.* Abstraction involves the process that attaches the particular to a larger related category or concept. Abstraction simplifies, and, at the same time, expands the perception and reality of the particular. Many years ago, Kurt Goldstein (1940) concluded, on the basis of his studies of the effects of brain damage on human functioning, that ability for abstract thinking is a necessary component of mental health. Abstraction fosters integration of thoughtful and proactive (confrontational) approaches to problems. Conversely, concreteness promotes segmentation of perception and passive adaptation. Too often in conflict situations people are advised to make the nature of the conflict practical so that it can be dealt with in concrete and segmented ways. I believe that a segmented situational approach to conflict often serves only to eliminate the conflict and does little to achieve an elimination of the source of the conflict. The latter requires abstraction, not concretization. Abstraction, which yields a comprehensive view of the conflict, is the underpinning of a healthy approach to proactive and radical intervention. My research has indicated that non-confrontation (conflict avoidance) is associated with concreteness and a segmented approach to issues (Abdennur, 1987). Defining complex conflicts as practical "problems" entails reliance on certain epistemological assumptions that can distort the understanding of the issue (see the section on conflict reconciliation in Chapter 4). Comprehensiveness addresses the direct (micro) and indirect social (macro) implications as well as the short- and long-term implications. Comprehensive understanding should be sought *before* seeking solutions.

3. *Construction of Self as Agent of Dignity and Honour.* Honour and dignity are abstract conceptions in which prosocial values are held

as part of the self and in a forthright manner. Thus, values that are part of honour are self-confronting and self-monitoring and also confrontative to others with respect to prosocial values.

4. *Addressing the Right Concern to the Right Party.* The objective conceptualization of a concern and its direction to the responsible party are central to the confrontational strategy. Sometimes concerns are expressed to the wrong party, emotions are expressed instead of addressing the issue, and individuals are confronted to avoid the issue.

The manager can explain to his or her staff the importance of confrontational approaches in curtailing the spread of camouflaged aggression. The cultivation of confrontation as an intellectual approach, as an ethic, as a method, and, ultimately, as an integral part of one's character is the most viable approach to addressing conflict within the organization.

Balancing the Two Modes at the Practical Level

The following steps provide a breakdown of the recommended intervention strategy. In keeping with the cognitive approach, the stress here is on the proper identification and conceptualization of aggression. Thus, the identification of behaviour, victim, injury, and perpetrator presented below are introduced from a cognitive rather than an inquisitional or litigious perspective. The main goal of the recommended strategy is to allow members of the organization to critically analyze their mode of aggression and then to confront the problem, the issue, and each other in a courteous manner to resolve conflict. By the same token, individuals who are unduly challenging, rude, or abrasive should be encouraged to adopt a civil manner. Also, specific recommendations (the "how to")— whether they are commonsensical or research based—are avoided because, as indicated before, the forms vary immensely with respect to individuals and situations, and because incumbents can deal with them effectively and creatively when the whole picture is clear and when they rely on basic wisdom.

1. Identification of the Behaviour

Initially, the act of aggression needs to be identified in isolation from its causes and from the intended victim. Second, the intention behind the act should be focused on and assessed in terms of level of consciousness, and in relation to matters of routine, chance, incompetence, or feigned incompetence. Third, the aggressive behaviour should be considered in the context of its broader organizational and social context.

2. Labelling of the Behaviour

Attaching an appropriate and catchy term or label to a particular form of camouflaged aggression can speed up the process of recognizing it as such. When such labels become publicly used, they may serve to deter people from engaging in behaviour associated with the term. Furthermore, well-chosen labels can help to identify the behaviour as antisocial and lead to appropriate administrative sanctions. Moreover, such identification may also serve to encourage victims to challenge the aggression.

Familiar terms such as "rumour mongering," "back stabbing," "passive-aggression" are useful labels. A term advanced in this study is *camouflaged aggression*. The term identifies the behaviour in question as masked and hidden and connotes ethological links to earlier and lower species. The concept of *mode* in aggression, together with the concepts of *confrontational mode, non-confrontational mode,* and *modal imbalance,* have a heuristic labelling value. *Modal shift* refers to the tactical shift from confrontation to non-confrontation, and conversely, in order to contain aggression and maximize deterrence. Equally useful concepts are *quantum of aggression, resonance of aggression,* and *warehousing of aggression* within the organization.

Being on the receiving end of camouflaged aggression as a result of personal or situational vulnerability can well be referred to as *hydraulic victimization*. *Position vulnerability* is used in reference to conditions where the structure of the position creates a point of low resistance that can lead to victimization. *Position victimology* refers to the general research concern of position vulnerability. The term *malignant aggression*, which refers to aggression generated by the need for the release of tension through some convenient target, is a useful construct that can be communicated by analogy to cancer. *Organizational foliage* refers to the intricate structures behind which aggressors seek camouflage and which gives rise to a need to flush them out into the clearing of personal responsibility.

The following are examples of other labels that can be employed. For someone who uses the common technique of withdrawing attention or affection by shifting unpredictably between warmth and coolness, the term *yo-yoing* may be applied; for one engaging in anxiety-provoking practices—*carpet pulling*; for the rationalizing of a personally motivated decision in terms of organizational needs and restrictions—*decision laundering*; for the dissemination of harmful information—*dusting*. A glossary of the concepts and labels introduced in this book is at the end of the book.

3. Identification of the Victim

Victims of camouflaged aggression may not be able to identify various forms of camouflaged aggression as aggressive and may misattribute the experienced distress to other sources, including their own failings or shortcomings. Sometimes the organization as a whole is blamed for the distress; at other times, the victim shoulders the blame ("It's my fault, I should have…"). Sometimes the victim simply blames happenstance or bad luck. Prompt victim identification will mobilize the intended victim's defences and may provoke guilt or intimidation in the aggressor, which, in both cases, may serve as a deterrent.

Victimization in camouflaged aggression is not confined to individuals who are the direct targets of such aggression. Because of the chains of structured interaction in organizations and the tendency to displace aggression, other individuals, including those outside of the organization, may be victimized.

The organization itself and society may be the victims. A holistic view of victimization requires going well beyond the individual victim. In North America the prevalent perspective of social atomism has led to a view of society as the aggregate of independent individuals or groups. This view downplays the idea of society as an all-encompassing entity that has its own rights that need to be protected, and that can influence the behaviour of individuals. "Victimless crime" is an example of a harmful notion based on an atomistic conception of society. Crimes committed with the consent of participating individuals (e.g., substance abuse, prostitution, gambling), according to this perspective, should be considered as victimless. However, even though the perpetrators may appear to be only harming themselves, their actions may ultimately be harmful to society. These individuals may have merited their suffering, but society may also be the victim of their self-indulgence, not only because of the social costs involved in providing services for them but also because their behaviour can be emulated and normalized, thus impacting social values.

4. Identification of the Injury

Following the identification of the victim, an assessment of injury becomes necessary. Three major categories of injury can be distinguished:

1. *Injury sustained by the individual.* This includes direct physical harm to the body; physical illness due to stress, emotional distress and suffering; deterioration in mental health, such as increased emotional vulnerability and loss of cognitive ability. Also included is injury sustained to one's sense of honour, dignity, self-esteem, and reputation.

2. *Injury sustained by the organization.* This includes absenteeism, vandalism, sabotage, decreased efficiency and productivity, an increase in the quantum of aggression, demoralization and decline in the quality of interpersonal relationships, decline in reputation and in profits.

3. *Injury sustained by society.* This involves the weakening of the public trust and allegiance to social institutions; demoralization and apathy in interpersonal relationships; defensive and paranoid withdrawals among people; self-centredness and loss of commitment to moral values, and subsequent decline in social cohesiveness.

5. Identification of the Perpetrator

The identification of the perpetrator and the laying of responsibility is the final step in the identification part of the intervention process. Regardless of whether an employee engages in camouflaged aggression for the purpose of self-protection, as retaliation for being victimized, or due to incompetence, he or she is still a perpetrator. Perpetrators are often shielded from detection by organizational foliage. Their detection requires an organizational commitment to fully investigate the sources of friction among its members and an organizational refusal to be beguiled by deception. It also requires an administrative resolve to make employees responsible for their behaviour.

After identifying a perpetrator, a manager may also need to confront and neutralize the perpetrator's repertoire of rationalizations. Rationalizations are often used to present the camouflaged aggression as an unavoidable by-product of office operations or as a way of furthering the interests of the organization. The form of rationalization which I refer to as *decision laundering* should not be allowed to "wash" within the work setting. These steps of identification and unmasking should be completed before the manager proceeds to reconciliatory interventions among the conflicting parties.

It must be stressed that the explicit intervention by management against acts of camouflaged aggression will gradually create a group dynamic among staff; in effect, it will motivate them to instinctively identify and deter perpetrators. Moreover, by adopting a comprehensive conceptualization of aggression and victimization, the organization will become a learning medium that mobilizes analytical and critical thinking with respect to camouflaged aggression.

6. Reduce Learning and Transmission of Camouflaged Aggression

Camouflaged aggression can be learned and transmitted through interpersonal interactions whereby, as discussed before in the context of social learning, an individual learns the techniques of carrying out a behaviour and learns the rationalizations and norms that legitimate its use. Key educators in this learning process are often senior ranking administrators who serve as models for copying and emulation.

In many organizations those most accomplished in camouflaged aggression often rise to the top, where their interpersonal style is emulated by those who aspire to their positions. Many are very diplomatic individuals who seem to get along well with others and are able to reduce friction within the organization because they are always able to "smooth things over." Upper management may need to identify these individuals and limit their influence, or get rid of them entirely.

Administrators are often propelled by a narcissistic need to recruit personnel who resemble them in style and orientation. Thus, one intervention strategy would be to not to allow these "educators" to hire their own staff in order to prevent the "self-duplication" process. Another strategy would be to bring in as their main assistants individuals with strong personalities who have a confrontational, open style.

7. Discourage the Hidden Agenda

A common strategy during meetings is for individuals to mask their true positions by expressing a position different from their own, or by expressing no position at all. This strategy is often tolerated on the ground that members have different views, and that dissent needs to be tolerated. Hidden agenda manoeuvring may be associated with superior intelligence or based on a fantasy in which an individual plays the role of the powerful leader who employs hidden agendas in service of higher goals. For example, mayors of small towns can become swamped with proposals for unrealistic schemes presented by municipal counsellors for the sake of exaggerating their importance or "connections." In such meetings, fake proposals are sometimes presented for the purpose of fishing for information regarding the positions of other members.

The hidden agenda strategy limits access to objective facts. This practice prolongs meetings and disputes, delays solutions, promotes suspicion and paranoia, and thwarts creative thinking, a process which thrives on authenticity and objectivity.

Managers should require an open declaration of the true concerns and opinions of those in attendance at meetings in order to arrive at well-defined items for discussion. This declaration is similar to that of Max Weber who recommended that scholars declare explicitly their value assumptions before embarking on their studies. An "unhidden agenda" policy requires the objective presentation of all positions and the presence of frank discussion.

8. Encourage Civility

Rude and discourteous verbal communication are not tolerated in most white-collar workplaces. Courtesy and good manners can be seen as a form of healthy camouflage. As ritualized and positively rewarded behaviour, good manners assume functions that can both control and sublimate (reduce) aggression.

In addition to controlling and sublimating aggression, good manners have another important function: they act as formal boundaries that protect the self from undue encroachments. As discussed in Chapter 2, good manners provide a level of protection by ensuring the individual is treated with dignity in accordance with values contained in the abstract categories such as a human being, a colleague, a neighbour, or a team member. Casualness, as opposed to formality, removes the individual from abstract boundaries in the interest of promoting spontaneity, authenticity, and the impression of equality in interactions. However, if casualness increases unduly, it can become more problematic than stuffy formality. A casual style can compromise the protective boundaries of the self in terms of physical and psychological distance, privacy, and respect for status and reputation; it can also render the individual vulnerable to manipulation under the façade of friendliness. These masked encroachments on dignity and status may result in uneasiness and interpersonal conflicts, even if all parties willingly adopt a casual style. I would describe some of the current forms of casualness that violate the formal protective boundaries of the self as antisocial behaviour. Thus, a formula presents itself: *If you want to promote civility, seek to limit casualness.*

I once knew a director of a college who required his professors to wear neckties year round (with short-sleeve shirts in hot summers) in order to affirm, symbolically, the distinction that professors are not students, and in order to defy the rampant trend of casualness. I also knew a manager of construction sites in the United Arab Emirates who insisted his workers communicate in a civil manner. For example, he required them to greet one another and to refrain from yelling and swearing; he also made them distribute food and drinks to one another in a respectful manner. He believed that overtly aggressive and disrespectful communication and excessive "kidding" can reduce cooperation and efficiency.

Intervention Focusing on Abnormal Personality Functioning

The personality orientation of directors, managers, and members is a main factor in the generation and augmentation of camouflaged aggression. Intervention must take into consideration abnormal personality features and their impact.

Neurotic Disorders

Neurotic traits such as compulsive orderliness and workaholism can generate tension, frustration, and grudges in those who must interact with such individuals. Some neurotic individuals who are motivated toward self-improvement can, through counselling, be made sensitive to their shortcomings. In many cases, however, intervention must also include measures to identify such neurotic individuals and then to protect them from their vulnerabilities. One of their most common vulnerabilities is a high level of anxiety; this can be easily provoked or augmented by certain managerial practices. Self-esteem is tied to a sense of security, with the latter affected by anxiety. Thus, highly anxious individuals should not be allowed to work under insensitive or non-empathetic managers, particularly those with passive-aggressive personality disorder.

Anxiety and low self-esteem can combine to generate camouflaged aggression in managers who are promoted to positions with considerable power and privilege, causing feelings of unworthiness and insecurity. The Peter Principle (Peter & Hull, 1970) maintains that, in a hierarchical system, an individual will likely be promoted to the level of his or her incompetence. A psychological version of the Peter Principle would suggest that an individual will likely be promoted to his or her level of insecurity. The anxiety experienced by such new incumbents often causes them to attack the status and self-worth of subordinates (i.e., they engage in *ego bashing*).

A common passive-aggressive technique used by neurotics is that of affect withdrawal. Some individuals who may have, in their early life, been subjected to affect withdrawal as a form of control reproduce the pattern in their later lives. These individuals indulge others with "tenderness and love" only to withdraw their investment by means of coolness, indifference, and avoidance. This technique of camouflaged aggression, which was discussed in Chapter 3, fosters generalized feelings of anxiety, depression, and paranoia. Confronting perpetrators with their behaviour can be effective in cases where the passive-aggression is neurotically based.

A subtle form of camouflaged aggression stems from the neurotic need for self-punishment, often expressed as a fear of success or as failure after success. There is also an aggressive component to self-inflicted failure in cases where one's failure can also hurt others. The typical overt approach is an enthusiastic exertion of effort towards the realization of a viable project, followed by decisions or other moves that cause the venture to collapse once success is imminent. These "mistakes" may not be accidental; the individuals may be unconsciously motivated to fail. In such cases, the aggression appears at first glance to be directed solely against the self and to be limited to the individual, particularly in cases where he or she is the sole proprietor of the enterprise. However, closer analysis often reveals that others suffer as a result of the individual's lack of success. Sometimes the accompanying victims are close individuals such as family members and business partners. Within organizations, other individuals and the organization as a whole can be victimized. The fact that these "failures" become victims themselves lessens their feelings of guilt for the suffering of others. Their personal losses mask the behaviour as an unintended mistake rather than an act of camouflaged aggression on self, colleagues, and organization. It is difficult to spot such individuals directly; however, an examination of their history often reveals a string of such projects. These individuals need to be counselled regarding their destructive behaviour and how it makes others, not just themselves, suffer.

A related form of self-injurious behaviour is seen in individuals who, with or without awareness, suppress their aggressive impulses against others and turn their aggressiveness against themselves in ways which do not appear to be aggressive but can be self-destructive. They behave like the professional golfers who blow their leads in major tournaments at the final holes through poor shots or poor decisions, which they would not normally be expected to make. As suggested before, the organization provides extensive opportunities for the delivery of such self-directed aggression. The awareness of this unhealthy dynamic can help in reducing it.

Personality Disorders

The ideal intervention strategy in the case of personality disorders should not be intervention, it should be *extinction*. When an incumbent is recognized as exhibiting one of the major personality disorders, measures to remove that individual from the position should be taken promptly. In fact, studies have shown that the number of employees fired for personality-related issues is far greater than those fired for incompetence. If the removal of that individual is not feasible, then the containment of his or her sphere of activity becomes the second alternative. Removing the employee who exhibits features (mild, severe, or mixed) of a disordered personality from a decision-making capacity and from close and intense interaction with others will reduce the effects of their antisocial behaviour, but it may not curtail it. For example, arranging for someone with a passive-aggressive or a paranoid personality disorder to work alone may not fully solve the problem. They can still deliver and provoke aggression through a variety of ways, particularly through electronic networks. A third alternative would be to explicitly institute punitive measures for any infraction they commit and to carry out such actions consistently. This strategy may work with passive-aggressive individuals who are responsive to explicit threats (creating a modal shift). Psychopathic individuals can be kept in line at least for some time by means of enforced threats of loss of privileges.

The intervention strategy may differ depending on whether the disordered employee is a manager or a coworker, but the psychological dynamics remain the same. For example, Babiac and Hare (2006) describe certain red flags for narcissistic and psychopathic personalities in the workplace: inability to form a team, inability to share, inability to act predictably, inability to accept blame, inability to tell the truth, and inability to act without aggression. The authors make the following recommendations on how to deal with a psychopathic boss:

build a reputation as a good performer, insist communications be put in writing, organize and make use of performance appraisals, avoid confrontations with the boss, and then make a formal complaint.

It may be possible to balance the problem individual's style by exploiting it to benefit the organization. But this need to be done *only within a specific setting and for a limited time.* A psychopath may do an exceptionally efficient job on a selling consignment. A narcissist may invest a great deal of energy and effort in a new venture or position that affords him or her the promise of self-aggrandizement. Someone with a histrionic personality disorder may perform superbly in a public relations job for a limited time. A compulsive or avoidant personality may do well on a task that requires reclusiveness and routine. However, problems arise when we attempt to restrain these individuals in order to shift their performance in the right direction. It is exceedingly difficult to contain or get rid of these individuals after they have done "good work" for you. Their ingenuity at intimidation and blackmail is enormous and they end up costing more in time, energy, and agony than their contribution was worth. It is important to keep in mind that the balance sheet of the individual with a serious personality disorder will ultimately never shift in favour of the organization.

In most cases, personality disorders tend to be chronic and not amenable to amelioration. Protecting society by improving the quality of organizational behaviour is becoming more and more crucial. Efforts must be taken by management to minimize the presence of individuals with disordered personalities in organizations, particularly in public agencies.

Other Intervention Strategies

1. Establishing Avenues for Refutation

It is obvious that not all harm that is expressed through the operation of organizations is the result of aggression (i.e., deliberate action carried out by individuals for the purpose of harming others). Clients and members of an organization can be harmed as a result of great number of events and conditions, both internal and external to the organization. However, owing to the complexity of structures and to certain psychological factors, victims may attribute aggressive intentions to employees who are innocent. Therefore, it becomes important to be able to identify the innocence of employees entangled in a harm-causing organizational process. In keeping with the cognitive approach, this assessment of culpability can be aided by an understanding of the behaviours involved in the attribution of blame and revenge reactions.

Bies, Tripp, and Kramer (1997) describe three prototypic patterns of social perception that have been found to contribute to revenge behaviour in the workplace. The first pattern is a tendency to make *personalistic attributions* about the conduct of members, particularly those who occupy higher positions. It was demonstrated (see, e.g., Kramer, 1995) that individuals tend to make overly personalistic attributions when they feel self-conscious or are under evaluative scrutiny. These personalistic attributions can motivate retaliation. Two motives were identified by Bees and Tripp (1995): selfishness and malevolence. A selfish harm-doer causes harm for personal profit. A malevolent harm-doer causes harm for the sake of hurting a particular victim. Vindictiveness tends to increase when the latter kind of attribution is made.

A second pattern in the attribution of blame is the *biased punctuation of conflict.* This refers to a tendency of victims to construe the history of conflict with the other party as part of a pattern and precalculated design. This type of bias contributes to vindictiveness by providing justifications for retaliation and by generating self-fulfilling patterns of action-reaction between the parties. A third pattern which contributes to the perceived need to engage in retaliatory behaviour, according to the above authors, is the *exaggerated perception of conspiracy* associated with paranoid cognitions. Paranoid misperception leads to hypervigilance, which along with personalistic attribution and biased punctuation of conflict, leads to the overattribution and overreaction to benign organizational exchanges.

In the context of conspiracy thinking and paranoid expectations, I have proposed (Abdennur, 2014) another problematic reaction, namely, *conspiracy denial*. Conspiracy denial is the converse of conspiracy cognition, as counterphobia to phobia, and as Gestalt dismantling to Gestalt building. Conspiracy denial can become obsessive, resulting in generalized conspiracy debunking, which serves to compromise the adequate response to real conspiracies taking place in increasingly complex settings. Another danger of conspiracy denial is that, by dissipating the causal links leading to conspiracy perception, it denies the problem. Denial of problems can generate other problems, including the somatization of stress.

Management's understanding of perceptual distortions such as those described above will help put blame reactions in perspective, control generalized paranoia, and facilitate reconciliation between the conflicting parties. The strategy for managing blame and ensuring methods of recourse for establishing innocence is fundamentally a cognitive-educational strategy. This strategy dictates that managers increase, not restrict, the flow of information and ideas into and within the organization. They should ask questions and allow the employees to discuss them in friendly meetings and to work toward cooperative goals.

2. Reduce Bureaucratic Intransigence by Modal Balance

It was proposed in Chapter 2 that the camouflaged blending of the incumbent with the organization is motivated by two goals: 1) avoiding personal responsibility, and 2) achieving invincibility. Both goals are implicated with intransigence and will be the concern of this section. As the employee identifies with the formal organizational structure, he or she experiences a lowering in personal responsibility (vulnerability) and an increase in feelings of power as the result of being part of a larger, more credible, and more powerful entity. That sense of power, because it is experienced within the regressed context of camouflage, and because it involves the relinquishing of personal responsibility, cannot amount to an authentic, expansive, and self-sustaining power. Most often this sense of power is sustained by reaction formation against actual power-lessness and by pathological narcissism. Thus, in conflict situations we frequently observe bureaucrats barricaded behind their positions—intransigent, defiant, and ready to fight to the last organizational "soldier."

This bureaucratic intransigence can be illustrated by the highly publicized case of a research scientist, Chander P. Grover, against his employer, the National Research Council of Canada (NRC). Five years after Grover filed a complaint with the Canadian Human Rights Commission, the tribunal ruled in 1992 that his employer had discrim-inated against him in matters of employment on the basis of his racial origin. It took two additional court rulings (in 1992 and in 1993) to force the management of the NRC to comply with the tribunal order and implement the remedies ("The Cost of Fighting Back," 1993). However, a final resolution did not materialize, as the administra-tion sought to engage Grover in multiple incidental lawsuits, involving several federal labour boards and the Supreme Court of Canada, all of which rendered him unable to resume his work. The courts consistently ruled in Grover's favour, but arriving at a settlement was a protracted affair; the case lasted twenty seven years, with a cost estimated by his lawyers to be close to $40 million of taxpayers' money and, up till now (2020), is still unresolved. It appears that the administration deployed a concerted strategy of delay to deplete the complainant's finances, patience, and well-being. Many high-ranking administrators and poli-ticians, including members of parliament and cabinet ministers, were approached but they all managed to avoid intervening to help settle the case. Many commented that the defiant behaviour of the NRC's administrators was an indication that bureaucracy is invincible. This assessment may well be correct, at least in unimodal settings like those of the Grover case, where a form of bureaucratic strategy is employed to challenge a bureaucratic system. In this case, it was legality against entrenched legality: a legal suit against a legally responding entity, resulting in a sophisticated orchestration of protracted camouflaged aggression. If the initial resistance to settling the case were followed by efforts to personally identify the entrenched bureaucrats and expose them to the public eye, or to direct the wrath of the defendant's supporters (creating a modal shift), then their compliance would have been swift. To lose access to the confrontational mode can be sometimes costly in time, money, and justice.

The centring of aggression expression on the non-confrontational mode can also contribute to the development of an inflated and unrealistic perception of one's position as powerful. This inflated and narcissistic perception runs the risk of utterly collapsing when bluntly challenged by a reaction from the confrontational mode. Bureaucrats who may have a thorough command of the operations, legal under-pinnings, and the political intricacies of an important post may operationally define their reality in terms of these bureaucratic powers under their control. As a result, their sense of power runs the risk of progressing pathologically toward a narcissistic sense of omnipotence. I witnessed a case of an individual, on the losing end of a complicated lawsuit, who called his legally fortified bureaucratic opponent to tell him that he will not be pursuing further legal options but was planning to "rearrange his face." In response to the physical threat, the bureau-crat went into a state of shock and could not work or sleep until I was able to offer reassurances that his challenger would not be pursuing the physical option. Such drastic reactions take place when the bureaucratic structures preclude the dynamic balancing of the two modes and allow a dangerous inflation in the perception of one's institutional powers.

The illustration in support of modal balance made in Chapter 1, about public servants becoming prompt and courteous with the advent of a civil war, resembles the above two cases, and requires another look. The camouflaged aggression of the public servant during the civil war was deterred by the increased probability of a retaliatory punch in the nose by a client. However, it should be stressed that it is not only the promptness of the retaliation that resulted in the deterrent impact, it is also the shift in mode (*modal shift*). The promptness in the delivery of a sanction enhances its deterrent effect while delay weakens it. But bureaucratic sanctions can also be swift. Recourse to immediate complaining to a supervisor is also possible but may not have the same impact as a direct verbal or physical burst because a complaint is subject to manoeuvering while a punch or a swear word is not. Thus, the shift in mode in this case exerted the main deterrent impact.

A camouflaged bureaucratic quest for power tends to progress gradually toward an infinite (absolute) experience of power. Durkheim (1897/1951) described how psychosocial drives such as ambition, greed, and quest for power, unlike other needs, tend to move to extreme forms of expression, ones that are chronic and difficult to limit or contain. The confrontative mode, regardless of whether it verbal, emotional, or physical, is inherently oriented toward identifiable and finite expression. Thus, modal balancing also involves balancing the psychological forces belonging to experiencing the *finite* and the *infinite*.

3. Understanding Bureaucratic Avoidance of Responsibility

As discussed before, the camouflaged blending of the incumbent with the organization is motivated, in part, by the need to avoid responsibility. Responsibility in this case is avoided at two levels: 1) at the level of escaping or minimizing negative feedback for actions taken, and 2) at the level of avoiding having to take new action or having to "stick one's neck out." Three major causes for the avoidance of responsibility merit consideration: one stemming from the structured operations, such as competition, anxiety, passing the buck, and survival adaptations (e.g., as analyzed by Jackall, 1987, and presented in Chapter 2 of this volume); and the other stemming from a phylogenetically based regression toward a state of camouflage activated by the formal structures of the organization. For a comprehensive understanding of bureaucratic avoidance of responsibility, a third causal dimension should be included. This third source of avoidance of responsibility stems from certain *personality orientations* held by "normal" people. This includes the previously described conflict avoidant personality syndrome (Abdennur,

1987), conflict reconciling personality syndrome (Abdennur, 2014); and the minimal self (Lasch, 1984), all of which are discussed in Chapter 4.

All of the three causal domains (organizational, phylogenetic, personality-oriented) for avoiding responsibility noted above are usually implicated in such dysfunction. But the fashionable explanation is to blame only the first cause: the bureaucratic "system." Bureaucracy is widely conceived as a system of management associated with impersonality, red tape, passing the buck, emotional bluntness, and so on. This perspective, which endorses Wrong's (1961) conception of "over-socialized" humans, ignores the fact that organizations not only act on their employees, they also recruit them. Organizations select, reward, and promote certain types of individuals, and exclude from their ranks other types of individuals. Recruitment is seldom a choice between those who are qualified and those who are not, especially nowadays when the technically qualified are in abundance. Thus, personality differences are crucial in organizational decision-making despite the overall impact of bureaucratic structures. Furthermore, some of those personality differences differentially interact with the role structures in a variety of resonating accommodations.

The failure of bureaucrats to assume active responsibility and leadership, such as in the case of Grover, strongly points to the presence of bureaucratized conflict avoidants and minimalists. Government bureaucracy and public service agencies have been partial to hiring and promoting individuals with these personality orientations. It appears that, for reasons of political functionality, such individuals have been zealously recruited into and promoted within bureaucracies. They are chosen for their lack of challenging or boat-rocking conduct, their compliance with political correctness, and their endorsement of the status quo. Their dysfunctional impact is drastically felt during times of crisis, when responsible initiatives and leadership are required. In such conditions, they instead precipitate further calamities. Some claim that conflict avoidants and intellectual minimalists predominate in public bureaucracies because private enterprise tends to draw and absorb most of the confrontative types. This may be the case, but there are instances where the psychologically and intellectually castrated personality of a professional male is regarded as an asset within certain public sectors.

This recent trend of recruiting conflict avoidants, conflict reconcilers, minimalists, and survivalists into public institutions has been reversing the institutionalization of charisma. Traditionally, a positive correlation between a high bureaucratic or political office and an incumbent's personal charisma was a consistent expectation. Individuals promoted or recruited for senior managerial or political positions were expected to be more forceful, more principled, more self-confident, and more personally wholesome than their subordinates. With the selective recruitment of the above personality types in many North American public institutions, the positive correlation between charisma and the senior public office is withering away. Instead of expecting rank to embrace character, one can now expect non-commitment, over-tolerance, banality, casualness, manipulativeness, and behind-covering to be happily accommodated to rank. This trend can be seen as an institutional version of the "anti-hero" theme in drama, something I call the *institutionalization of anti-charisma*.

Combat Philosophy

Some authors (e.g., Sankar, 1994) endorse an ethical challenge to organizational deviance. The appeal to and the cultivation of a sense of ethicality is expected to have a mediating and prosocial impact on organizational behaviour. In a demonstration of his commitment to an ethical approach, Sankar lists the names of books advocating Machiavellian management but avoids citing the authors' names out of an apparent ethical disdain.

I believe that challenging camouflaged aggression from a predominantly ethical approach is ineffective for three reasons.

First, deviant behaviour can be distinguished from unethical behaviour because in the case of deviance the employee relies on societal rather than organizational standards to assess the unacceptable act (see, e.g.,

Robinson & Bennett, 1995). Societal and organizational norms may conflict, and under certain conditions deviant behaviour is not always unethical. These authors give the example of a company dumping toxic waste in a river, which may be seen as a deviant act from a societal perspective. However, the action of an employee who blew the whistle on the company would be viewed by colleagues as a violation of organizational norms. A similar ethical divergence may exist between front-desk management and upper management. Junior employees dealing directly with clients may be organized, reliable, polite, and ethical. But this ethicality may not apply to the upper echelons, who may be indulging in corrupt, unethical practices. An orderly and ethical front desk management may present a misleading impression of the total organization.

Second, ethical conduct is subject to personal relativity. Although ethical norms are abstract and generalizable, they do not have the binding power found in all-encompassing ideologies or belief systems. Ethical norms are vulnerable to personality deviations stemming from ambition, greed, and need for safety. Also, ethicality can be held for the purpose of bolstering the public image of a manager rather than as a sincere and universal commitment. As a result, ethical behaviour becomes contingent on situation.

Third, ethical norms are vulnerable to macro social and cultural changes. Economic changes, political conflicts, and dominant cultural trends can undermine the commitment to ethical standards. For example, the self-centredness found in a culture of narcissism can increase a sense of personal entitlement at the expense of ethical commitments. Ethicality as an individual commitment to prosocial organizational behaviour, if it is to be effective, needs to be guided and energized by dominant and stable sociocultural and ideological values.

This book argues that combatting camouflaged aggression should follow a three-dimensional strategy, referred to as a *cognitive strategy*, as part of the general *organizational and managerial wisdom* strategy discussed earlier.

1. A theoretical and comprehensive understanding of aggression in complex systems is essential. A cognitive approach is preferable to that of describing, classifying, and recommending "what to do" about the "problem." This theoretical understanding can lead to the recognition of aggressive behaviour in its particular expression and, at the same time, can help in inspiring wise intervention.

2. General constructs and intervention strategies, such as those suggested in this text, can help manage and reduce camouflaged aggression. They include modal balance; modal shift; proper identification of injury, perpetrator, and victim; discouraging hidden agendas; reducing transmission; redress; and dealing with personality disorders as a source of aggression.

3. The normative affirmation of confrontation.

Confrontational values comprise 1) objectivity, 2) rationality, 3) comprehensiveness, 4) direct expression of opposition, 5) proactiveness, 6) radicality in intervention, and 7) the abstract construction of self as an embodiment of dignity and honour. These values were traditionally held in high regard and were considered core values of masculinity. A nonsexist understanding of these core confrontative values, and an examination of their crucial role in the evolution of the human race and their present social functions with the explosive development of complex systems, is now most timely. No society can afford the demise of these seven pillars of confrontation.

A cognitively based confrontation strategy is recommended as a support for, or as an alternative to, the ethical approach. For example, the appeal to the value of honour and dignity is, like the appeal to ethicality, crucial to self-image and moral standing. But honour is more abstract than ethics, as it permeates all aspect of self. Its abstract status is manifested in the fact that it does not need an external audience to be activated; one finds it "beneath one's dignity" to behave in a sneaky or unjust manner. The sense of honour and dignity is sustained by healthy narcissism, and perhaps the recultivation of this sense of healthy narcissism may offset the effects of its pathological counterpart.

Without a strong allegiance to the values of confrontation, we risk, not only a rampant increase in camouflaged aggression but also a rapid plummet into a state of one-dimensional containment and total administration (Marcuse, 1964) and the demise of freedom and mental health.

EPILOGUE
Complexity, Camouflage, Entropy, and Explosive Violence

THE THEORETICAL MODEL presented in this book assumes
the bimodality of aggression expression. Despite variations in
the medium, organizational structure, interactive context, and
type of relationship between aggressor and victim, all expressions of aggression can be classified along the confrontation
and non-confrontation dimensions. In organizations, when
aggression is expressed excessively or exclusively through one
mode, the imbalance is likely to increase not only the number
of avenues in which aggression is expressed within that mode
but also the overall quantum of aggression. That is, modal
imbalance causes aggression to proliferate and increase,
while modal balance directs aggression toward containment.
Although modal imbalance in favour of confrontational aggression results in a speedy escalation of aggression, it quickly
becomes geared, particularly within organizations, toward
resolution and subsequent dissipation. The lack of openness
and consciousness that accompanies non-confrontational
aggression and its insidious spread precludes direct resolution
and allows the modal imbalance to increase the quantum of
aggression over long periods of time. It has been argued here
that the rapid proliferation of complex systems in contemporary society has created a vast number of structured

opportunities for the expression and delivery of aggression within the non-confrontational mode, including that of self-targetted destructiveness. The drastic increase in the number of organizational opportunities to deliver camouflaged aggression, together with anti-confrontational norms, is creating a modal imbalance in favour of camouflaged aggression. The surplus aggression can accumulate as potential energy, embodied in structural opportunities and in psychological dispositions adapted to these structures. The kinetic expression of this aggression takes three main forms: 1) increased conflicts (disorganization), 2) mental health problems, and 3) episodes of explosive violence. The preponderance of camouflaged aggression through social institutions can shift the overall quality of aggression and its expression in society toward the primordial strategy of camouflage. The camouflage strategy in humans tends to cultivate conflict avoidance (cowardice) and compromise proactive and radical intervention.

Complex Systems

Insect colonies, the human brain, the immune systems, large corporations, the economy, monetary systems, the stock market, and society itself are examples of complex systems. Baranger (2011) identified some of the typical properties of complex systems. He noted the following: 1) Complex systems contain many constituents often interacting nonlinearly; 2) The constituents of a complex system are interdependent; they impact other parts and the whole system; 3) A complex system is capable of developing and shaping behaviour; 4) The complex system is capable of learning and adaptating to its environment; 5) A system's complexity creates movement toward competition and chaos, which is usually balanced by a movement for order and cooperation imposed by its objectives; 6) Complex systems are open systems; and 7) Individual elements are often ignorant of the behaviour of the whole system in which they are imbedded. Thus, a complex system consists of a network of components that are separate, multiple, dynamically interacting, learning, and adapting, and that involve an interplay of chaos and order.

Camouflaged Aggression as a Complex System

When camouflaged aggression disperses through ever-growing structures and avenues of complex systems, it acquires the characteristics of complex systems itself. Its different expressions interact, resonate, dissipate, break down and then reorganize, spread both arithmetically and geometrically, and acquire momentum. Despite camouflaged aggression's almost infinite expressions, it can be seen as a self-organizing system predicated on the underlying goal of delivering harm. This is similar to the complex monetary system; it permeates diverse activities but maintains its primary function by facilitating the process of value exchange. Microtransactions emerge at the macro level as financial institutions and economic activity, as prosperity and recession. Similarly, the micro expressions of camouflaged aggression create impacts at the macro level in the form of criminality, political conflict, and mental health issues.

Entropy

"Entropy" refers to disorder in a changing system. The lower the available energy within a system to do useful work, the higher the entropy and disorder. Entropy is aggravated when energy can be transferred only in one direction: from an ordered state to a disordered state. Although the concept of entropy originated in the fields of thermodynamics and statistical mechanics, it has been applied in many areas, such as communications, economics, information science, and music. In social systems it is characterized by the depletion of available energy and increasing degrees of uncertainty, fragmentation, stagnation, and chaos. Such a process can be seen as a terminal stage in the life of a social system (Baranger, 2011).

As aggression is expressed through the structures of the formal system, the greater part of it becomes camouflaged. This masking complicates the process of its expression. Personality disorders and other conditions have particular dynamics which contribute to the incidence of aggression. The increasing availability of structural avenues for the expression of aggression (e.g., advanced technology) allows aggression to spread exponentially, pervasively, and chaotically. Thus, aggression in complex systems can easily fulfil the two conditions for entropy: chaos and one-directionality of energy. Entropy is thus manifested in 1) multiple, insidious, and amorphous forms of aggression that are largely beyond conscious monitoring; and 2) movement in one direction, namely, toward non-confrontation and away from conscious and normatively structured confrontation.

Explosive Violence

When aggression spreads into ever-changing and interacting avenues, it eventually accumulates and is expressed hydraulically (at the least resistant point); this process also contributes to chaos and entropy. In this state, aggression loses its conscious purposes. It becomes an alien force deprived of normative and other abstract structuring. It also becomes a form of tension release in a convenient situation. At this level of concreteness, aggression can only be expressed in a sporadic and malignant manner, and as explosive violence, such as that seen in random mass shootings.

It is a common observation among mental health professional that individuals with various types of mental illness or forms of brain damage do not express their aggression in a conscious, confrontative, strategic, and protracted manner. They express their aggression non-confrontationally as in passive-aggression, sporadic or short-lived emotional reactions, and explosive violence. That is, they are not capable of open battle; they are only capable of camouflaged aggression or violent outbursts. There are serious implications to the decline in open confrontation. This is discussed in my previous work on conflict avoidance (Abdennur, 1987), and is illustrated in the following quotation from that study:

The Romans had a saying: "If you want to prolong peace, prepare for war." In his book *The Biology of Peace and War* (1979), the eminent ethologist Irenäus Eibl-Eibesfeldt argued that "If you want to promote peace, study war." The research and theory presented in this book suggest an elaboration of the above recommendation: "If you want to promote peace, study not only war, but also, those incapable of war." (p. 128)

In conclusion, I suggest that camouflaged aggression, as it flows through the structures of complex systems, can itself be seen as a central complex system in contemporary society. It is like the monetary currency that flows through and permeates many domains and accumulates in certain places. The accumulation of quanta of non-confrontational aggression in social institutions and personalities of individuals can precipitate a state of entropy, evidenced as exhaustion, paralysis of radical will, and disorganization, affecting the whole of society.

The most visible effect of this deterioration, in my view, is the absence of effective political leadership in the world today. Humanity is facing immense challenges if it is to ensure its quality of life and ultimate survival. Meanwhile, the world is full of leaders who are incapable of taking radical action; they are only concerned with politicking, limited problem-solving, and harm reduction. Camouflaged aggression hides from battle but can precipitate blind explosive violence. The gun in the hands of a random murderer may be the controls to a nuclear weapon in the hands of a similar person. Only the true warrior can engage in conscious, protracted, and radically directed challenges; the non-warrior can only produce entropy or explosive violence. Those who are incapable of confrontation are the problem.

GLOSSARY

Concepts Advanced or Utilized in the Book

Aggression: Any action or inaction directed by an individual toward the conscious or unconscious goal of causing harm or suffering.

Anomic Aggression: Aggression committed without any reference to social values or sense of justice.

Anti-Organizational Personality Profile: An assertive profile combining, in a synergic manner, the following three traits: aggrandized ego, concrete thinking, and unethicality (arrogant, ignorant, and corrupt).

Balance Sheet in Personality Disorders: A measurement of the ratio between the negative and the positive input that an organization receives from an employee with a personality disorder assessed over a lengthy period of time. It is suggested that this ratio is ultimately not in favour of the organization and can be used as a diagnostic criterion for the presence of a personality disorder.

Bimodal Aggression: Aggression delivered through forms of behaviour belonging to the two modes: confrontational and non-confrontational.

Bureaucratic Avoidance of Responsibility: Avoidance of the negative repercussions of previous decisions and avoiding having to make new decisions through resorting to a camouflaged blending with the position.

Bureaucratic Intransigence: The stubborn and oppositional behaviour of a bureaucrat that involves challenging others by means of an organizational position and at the same time camouflaging the self with it.

Bureaucratic Sabotage: The disruption or the undermining of efficiency carried out by junior bureaucrats against their seniors, accomplished without actually breaking rules. Excessive rule-following and information-overloading are examples.

Camouflaged Aggression: Non-confrontational aggression expressed within the organization and employing its formal structures for the delivery and masking of the aggression.

Cathartic Release: The feeling of relief and the diminution in the need to further aggress following the expression of aggression. Confrontational aggression produces a faster cathartic release than non-confrontational aggression.

Conflict Avoidance Syndrome: A pervasive personality orientation in normally functioning individuals that consistently avoids polarization and conflict.

Conflict Reconciliation Syndrome: A pervasive personality orientation in normally functioning individuals that consistently seeks mediation of conflict and deal-making.

Confrontational Mode: Expression of aggression that is direct, active, and conscious, and where the intention, perpetrator, act, and target, are readily identifiable.

Confrontational Revenge vs. Getting Even: In the former, the victim directs his retaliatory action directly and overtly at the perpetrator, thus speeding conflict resolution and promoting deterrence. In the latter, the victim directs his revenge actions in a non-confrontational, protracted, displaced, and camouflaged manner, which fails to shorten conflict or promote deterrence.

Convergence on Injustice: The compliance with, or the cooperation of, employees in carrying out an unjust action against a client or a member of the organization.

Conspiracy Denial: The obsessive debunking of conspiracy assumptions that is propelled by a reaction formation against conspiracy thinking as in the case of counterphobia.

Functions of Camouflage: The first function is to protect the animal from being observed by a predator; the second is to facilitate efficient delivery of aggression for predation; the third to protect the predator from the defensive reaction of the prey. Organizational camouflage provides the bureaucrat with the same functions in a parallel manner.

Geometric Spread of Aggression: The progressive spread of aggression among the interacting members of an organization which results from the displacement of aggression from one individual onto several others, who in turn displace onto more individuals.

Honour vs. Vanity: Honour is an abstract and enduring definition of self, based on the incorporation of socially revered values within the self. It is experienced internally as self-respect; it is not amenable to self-deception. It is self-monitoring and is defended by healthy narcissism. Vanity is an alienated and more public version of honour. It is predominantly experienced externally as public image and is amenable to expedient presentation. It is less self-monitoring of behaviour than honour and is defended by pathological narcissism.

Hydraulic Principle of Aggression: Accumulated aggression that seeks expression at the point of least resistance.

Hydraulic Victimization: Becoming a victim of aggression as the result of occupying a point of least resistance due to personal or situational vulnerability.

Hydraulically Expressed Aggression: Aggression expressed at the point of least resistance.

Institutionalization of Anti-Charisma: The withering away of traditional positive association between rank and personal charisma as a result of the extensive hiring and promotion of conflict avoidants, minimalists, and survivalists.

Interpersonal Sabotage: The non-confrontational aggression expressed among closely interacting individuals such as friends and coworkers.

Malignant Aggression: Aggression propelled solely by the need for tension release and the presence of a convenient situation.

Medium of Aggression: The context of the expression and delivery of aggression, i.e., physical, verbal, emotional, and cognitive.

Minimal Self: Refers to Christopher Lasch's (1984) concept of constricted sense of self that primarily seeks survival, with minimal conditions placed on the quality of survival.

Modal Balance: The availability of options, avenues, and norms that permit the expression of aggression along both modes in a given context.

Modal Imbalance: The blockage of options, avenues, and norms belonging to one mode while those belonging to the other mode remain open and available in a given context.

Modal Shift: The response to aggression by means of methods belonging to the opposite mode. Appropriate modal shift can directly contribute to modal balance and to deterrence.

Mode of Aggression: Basic qualitative style of the expression of aggression. Two basic modes can be identified: the confrontational and the non-confrontational.

Neutralization of Conflict: The use of "civilized" office etiquette and interpersonal courtesy and "friendliness" to eliminate the overt and affective manifestations of conflict.

Non-Confrontational Mode: Expression of aggression that is indirect, passive, and oriented toward masking the intention, perpetrator, act, and target.

Oncological Model of Narcissism: The alienation of self-image under the impact of exhibitionism and its progressive development into an aggrandized public image that feeds on the individual's energy and impairs personal well-being, as would a cancerous tumour.

Paradox of Modern Life: The tendency of the contemporary formal organization, the most evolved social structure, to invoke, catalyse, and accommodate itself to the highly primitive strategy of camouflage.

Phylogenetic Regression Toward Camouflage: Operations within complex organizational structures that induce a regression along phylogenetic paths toward the primitive state of camouflage; characterized by exaggerated fear, hiding, and deception, and by the non-confrontational expression of aggression.

Porcupine Entanglement: Interaction with public agencies that are poorly managed or harbour disordered personalities, which can present a level of potential distress to a client. The client of such agencies risks a harmful interaction that is similar to a thorny entanglement with a porcupine.

Position Victimology: The study of a position's characteristics which contribute to the victimization of the individual who occupies the position.

Position Vulnerability: Characteristics of the position (not the individual incumbent) that present points of least resistance or weak deterrence (e.g., contract or part-time jobs).

Principle of Equivalence in Pathological Narcissism: The facility of the narcissist to support a goal and its demise at the same time, and thus reconcile constructiveness with destructiveness.

Pseudo-Confrontation: The use of an assertive interpersonal style to confront others while avoiding confrontation with the real issue.

Psychological Disarming: The neutralizing of the retaliatory hostility of a victim by means of interpersonal civility which allows the perpetrator to perpetuate his aggression under safer conditions.

Psycho-Structural Marriage: The adaptive compatibility between the needs and characteristics of an incumbent's personality and those of the position. In the case of disordered personalities, this compatibility "marriage" increases the motivation for the delivery of camouflaged aggression.

Quantity to Quality Conversion: The increase in the number of incumbents with disordered personality characteristics that leads to changes in the quality of interaction and operation within the organization.

Quantum of Aggression: The amount of expressed aggression among individuals in an interactive context, together with the potential individual dispositions and structured avenues available for the expression of aggression. The quantum of aggression can be present in both kinetic and potential states.

Regressed Aggression: Aggression with one or more of the following characteristics: hydraulically expressed, malignant, anomic, and camouflaged.

Resonance of Aggression: The amplification in the quantum of aggression beyond what is expected from a certain stimulus. This amplification results from the stimulus targetting a personal vulnerability of an individual or from an individual being targetted by multiple sources of aggressive stimuli within the organization.

Self-Directed Aggression in Organizations: Organizations increase and proliferate avenues for the delivery of aggression against others and against self. Self-destructiveness increases with the increase of structured opportunities that can be used for self-sabotage.

Unimodal Aggression: Aggression delivered through forms of behaviour that are restricted to one mode. This restriction is personally or structurally imposed or both.

Violence: Use of physical force to injure or harm. A form of aggression expressed through a physical medium and often within the confrontational mode.

Warehousing of Aggression: The accumulation of aggression as individual dispositions to aggress and as structured opportunities for the delivery of aggression within the organization. Aggression is stored both as potential and kinetic energy.

Basic Techniques of Camouflaged Aggression

Bureaucratic Vendetta: The perseverance of retaliatory intention in a lowered or suspended state of affect; characterized by waiting and timing.

Control by Overwork: The overwhelming of the attention of employees by excessive work demands, rendering them less capable of engaging in criticism and office politics. In order to ensure compliance, the excessive work demands need to be relevant to the advancement of the employee's career and need to be well compensated.

Ego Bashing: The attack on an employee's core self, status, or self-worth, as distinguished from attacks on extensions of self in terms of the employee's productivity, management style, or decisions.

Entrapment: The luring of a victim in some beguiling way, such as displaying fake warmth and understanding, into suspending his or her self-protective behaviour.

Inaccessibility: The use of legitimate techniques available in an organization to avoid or postpone direct contact with a client or a member of the organization.

Indecision: Tendency toward decision avoidance, reflecting psychological insecurity and a technique for camouflaged aggression. In the latter case indecision can be used to frustrate, exacerbate, and demoralize others.

Information Manipulation: The use of bureaucratic procedure to aggress by disseminating, withholding, building, and timing information.

Non-Interference: The deliberate ignoring of an employee who is unwittingly committing a mistake.

Random Kindness: The unexpected and extravagant help given by a manager to an employee or client who may not have asked for it. This act of kindness is often intended to neutralize the perpetrator's previous negative deeds, to present a positive image, or to spite an adversary or victim.

Rigidity: The use of bureaucratic procedure to block change and to thwart innovative ideas.

Subordination via Sexualization: The display of sexual attractiveness to enhance power and charisma over a client or coworker. This is consistent with the social exchange theory of power.

Time Manipulation: The use of bureaucratic procedure to aggress by rushing people or by delaying them.

Undermining the Sense of Security: The use of a variety of anxiety-provoking procedures for the purpose of undermining the sense of security of employees. A state of insecurity can make employees compliant and vulnerable to manipulation.

Waiting as a Status Degradation Ceremony: The demoralization and loss of self-esteem of a client from having to wait for a long time to see an official by appointment.

Withdrawal: The use of withdrawal of attention and of positive affect to induce anxiety, confusion, and lowered self-esteem in an employee.

Labels for Some Forms of Camouflaged Aggression

Affectional Yo-Yoing: The intermittent display of emotion which involves shifting unpredictably between affectivity and coolness.

Carpet Pulling: Engaging in anxiety-provoking practices.

Decision Laundering: The rationalization of a personally motivated decision in terms of the organization's needs and restrictions.

Dusting: The dissemination of harmful information.

Organizational Foliage: A metaphor taken from the natural world; refers to the intricate organizational structures where aggressors take cover.

Withdrawal of Love: Deliberate withdrawal of attention and affect from someone.

REFERENCES

Abdennur, A. (1987). *Conflict resolution syndrome: Volunteerism, violence and beyond.* Ottawa: University of Ottawa Press.

Abdennur, A. (2000). *Camouflaged aggression: The hidden threat to individuals and organizations.* Calgary: Detselig.

Abdennur, A. (2013). Status inconsistency, narcissism, and ego bashing in the workplace: A theoretical model. *International Journal of Criminology and Sociological Theory, 6*(4), 181–90.

Abdennur, A. (2014). *The Arab mind: An ontology of abstraction and concreteness* (2nd ed.). Ottawa: Kogna Publishing.

Alkarni, S. (2017). Personal communication.

American Psychiatric Association. (1987). *Diagnostic and statistical manual of mental disorders* (3rd ed., revised). Washington, DC: Author.

American Psychiatric Association. (1994). *Diagnostic and statistical manual of mental disorders* (4th ed.). Washington, DC: Author.

American Psychiatric Association. (2013). *Diagnostic and statistical manual of mental disorders* (5th ed.). Washington, DC: Author.

Atallah, S. (1976, September 18). *Al-Nahar* (daily newspaper: main editorial.) Beirut: Lebanon.

Babiak, P., & Hare, R. (2006). *Snakes in suits: When psychopaths go to work.* New York: Regan Books.

Bandura, A. (1986). *Social foundations of thought and action: A socio-cognitive view.* Englewood Cliffs, NJ: Prentice-Hall.

Baranger, M. (2011). *Chaos, complexity, and entropy*. Cambridge, MA: Complex Systems Institute.

Baron, R.A. (1977). *Human aggression*. New York: Plenum Press.

Bennis, W. (1966). *Changing organizations: Essays on the development and evolution of human organization*. New York: McGraw Hill.

Berkowitz, L. (1962). *Aggression: A social psychological analysis*. New York: McGraw Hill.

Berkowitz, L. (1989). The frustration-aggression hypothesis: An examination and reformulation. *Psychological Bulletin, 106*(1), 59–73.

Berkowitz, L., Cochran, S.T., & Embree, M.C. (1981). Physical pain and the goal of aversively stimulated aggression. *Journal of Personality and Social Psychology, 40*(4), 687–700.

Bies, R., & Tripp, T. (1996). Beyond distrust: "Getting even" and the need for revenge. In R. Kramer & T. Tyler (Eds.), *Trust in organizations: Frontiers of theory and research* (pp. 246–60). Newbury Park, CA: Sage.

Bies, R., Tripp, T., & Kramer, R. (1997). At the breaking point: Cognitive and social dynamics of revenge in organizations. In R. Giacalone & J. Greenberg (Eds.), *Antisocial behavior in organizations* (pp. 18–36). Thousand Oaks, CA: Sage.

Bowling, N., & Hershcovis, S. (Eds.). (2017). *Research and theory on workplace aggression*. Cambridge, UK: University Cambridge Press.

Buss, A.H. (1961). *The psychology of aggression*. New York: Wiley.

Buss, A.H. (1971). Aggression pays. In J.L. Singer (Ed.), *The control of aggression and violence: Cognitive and physiological factors* (pp. 7–18). San Diego, CA: Academic Press.

Caplan, R.D. (1987). Person-environment fit theory: Commensurate dimensions, time perspectives, and mechanisms. *Journal of Vocational Behavior, 31*(3), 248–67.

Capozzoli, T., & McVey, R. (1966). *Managing violence in the workplace*. Delray Beach, FL: St. Lucie Press.

Christie, R., & Geis, F. (1970). *Studies in Machiavellianism*. New York: Academic Press.

Cleckley, H. (1976). *The mask of sanity: An attempt to clarify some issues about the so-called psychopathic personality* (5th ed.). St. Louis, MO: Mosby.

Clemson, U. (1994). Employee sabotage: A random or preventable phenomenon? *Journal of Managerial Issues, 6*(3), 311–30.

Cost of fighting back. (1993, July 24). *Ottawa Citizen.*

Daft, R.L. (1989). *Organization theory and design.* St. Paul, MN: West Publishing.

DeLara, E. (2016). *Bullying scars: The impact on adult life and relationships.* Oxford, UK: Oxford University Press.

Duffy, M., & Sperry, L. (2014). *Overcoming mobbing: A recovery guide for workplace aggression and bullying.* Oxford, UK: Oxford University Press.

Durkheim, É. (1951). *Suicide: A study in sociology.* New York: Free Press. (Original work published in 1897).

Eibl-Eibesfeldt, I. (1979). *The biology of peace and war: Men, animals, and aggression.* London: Thames and Hudson.

Eibl-Eibesfeldt, I. (1989). *Human ethology: The biology of behaviour.* New York: Aldine de Gruyter.

Fairholm, G.W. (1993). *Organizational power politics: Tactics in organizational leadership.* New York: Praeger.

Feher, F., & Heller, A. (1982). The antinomies of peace. *Telos, 53,* 5–16.

Feshbach, S., & Singer, R. (1957). The effects of personal and shared threats upon social prejudice. *Journal of Abnormal and Social Psychology, 54*(3), 411–16.

Feuerbach, L. (1957). *The essence of Christianity.* New York: Harper, 1957. (Original work published in 1841).

Frank, M.A. (2017). *The porcupine effect: Pushing others away when you want to connect.* Branson West, MO: Excel At Life.

Freud, S. (1958). *Beyond the pleasure principle.* Oxford, UK: Oxford University Press. (Original work published in 1920).

Freud, S. (1961). *Civilization and its discontents.* New York: W.W. Norton. (Original work published in 1930).

Freud, S. (1964). *Moses and monotheism.* London: Hogarth Press. (Original work published 1938).

Freud, S. (1965). *Introductory lectures in psychoanalysis.* New York: W.W. Norton. (Original work published in 1917).

Fromm, E. (1955). *The sane society.* New York: Holt, Rinehart & Winston.

Giacalone, R.A., & Greenberg, J. (Eds.). (1997). *Antisocial behavior in organizations.* Thousand Oaks, CA: Sage.

Goldstein, K. (1940). *Human nature in the light of psychopathology.* Cambridge, MA: Harvard University Press.

Goodall, J. (1965). *Through a window: My thirty years with the chimpanzees of Gombe*. Boston, MA: Houghton Mifflin.

Griffin, G.R. (1991). *Machiavelli on management: Playing and winning the corporate power game*. New York: Praeger.

Hammer, M., & Champy, J. (1993). *Reenginering the corporation: A manifesto for business revolution*. New York: Harper.

Hare, R.D. (1970). *Psychopathy: Theory and research*. New York: John Wiley.

Hare, R.D. (1991). *The Hare psychopathy checklist–revised*. Toronto, ON: Multi-Health Systems.

Hare, R.D. (1993). *Without conscience: The disturbing world of the psychopaths among us*. New York: Simon & Schuster.

Hare, R.D., & Schalling, D. (Eds.) (1978). *Psychopathic behaviour: Approaches to research*. New York: John Wiley.

Harrington, A. (1972). *Psychopaths*. New York: Simon & Schuster.

Hershcovis, M.S. (2011). "Incivility, social undermining, bullying...Oh my": A call to reconcile constructs within workplace aggression research. *Journal of Organizational Behavior, 32*(3), 499–519.

Homans, G.C. (1961). *Social behavior: Its elementary forms*. New York: Harcourt.

Immelmann, K. (Ed.). (1977). *Encyclopedia of ethology*. New York: Van Nostrand.

Jackall, R. (1987). The moral ethos of bureaucracy. In R. Glassman, W. Swatos, & P. Rosen (Eds.), *Bureaucracy against democracy and socialism*. New York: Greenwood Press.

Jackall, R. (1988). *Moral mazes: The world of corporate managers*. Oxford, UK: Oxford University Press.

Jones, D.A. (2013). The morality and ethics of workplace revenge: Avengers' moral considerations and the consequences of revenge for stakeholder well-being. In R.A. Giacalone & M.D. Promislo (Eds). *Handbook of unethical work behavior: Implications for individual well-being* (pp. 56–72). Armonk, NY: M.E. Sharpe.

Jordan, J., & Sternberg, R.J. (2007). Wisdom in organizations: A balance theory analysis. In E.H. Kessler & J.R. Bailey (Eds.), *Handbook of organizational and managerial wisdom* (pp. 3–18). Thousand Oaks, CA: Sage.

Kelleher, M.D. (1967). *Profiling the lethal employee: Case studies of violence in the workplace*. Westport, CT: Praeger.

Kernberg, O.F. (1984). *Severe personality disorders: Psychotherapeutic strategies.* New Haven, CT: Yale University Press.

Kessler, E.H., & Bailey, J.R. (Eds.). (2007). *Handbook of organizational and managerial wisdom.* Thousand Oaks, CA: Sage.

Knepp, K.A.F. (2012). Understanding student and faculty incivility in higher education. *The Journal of Effective Teaching, 12*(1), 32–45.

Kohlberg, L. (1969). *Stages in the development of moral thought and action.* New York: Holt, Rinehart & Winston.

Kramer, R.M. (1995). The distorted view from the top: Power, paranoia and distrust in organizations. In R. Bies, R. Lewicki, & B. Sheppard (Eds.), *Organizations and nation states: New perspective on conflict and cooperation.* San Francisco, CA: Jossey-Bass.

Lange, A.J., & Jakubowski, P. (1978). *Responsible assertive behavior: Cognitive/ behavioral procedures for trainers.* Champaign, IL: Research Press.

Lasch, C. (1979). *The culture of narcissism: American life in an age of diminishing expectations.* New York: Warner Books.

Lasch, C. (1984). *The minimal self: Psychic survival in troubled times.* New York: W.W. Norton.

Leiter, M.P., Peck, E., & Baccardax, A. (2017). Combating workplace aggression via organizational intervention. In N.A. Bowling & M.S. Hershcovis (Eds.). *Research and theory on workplace aggression* (pp. 322–49). Cambridge, UK: Cambridge University Press.

Lewin, K. (1952). *Field theory in social science: Selected theoretical papers.* Ed. D. Cartwright. London: Tavistock.

Leymann, H. (1996). The content and development of mobbing at work. In D. Zapf and H. Leymann (Eds.), *Mobbing and victimization at work* (pp. 165–84). New York: Edwin Mellen Press.

Li, X., & Lim, S. (2017). Cross-cultural differences in workplace aggression. In N.A. Bowling & M.S. Hershcovis (Eds.), *Research and theory on workplace aggression* (pp. 245–68). Cambridge, UK: Cambridge University Press.

Lipinski, J., & Crothers, L.M. (Eds.). (2014). *Bullying in the workplace: Causes, symptoms, and remedies.* London, UK: Routledge.

Lord, M.P. (1986). *Macmillan dictionary of physics.* New York: Macmillan.

Lorenz, K. (1966). *On aggression.* London, UK: Methuen & Co.

Lorenz, K. (1981). *The foundations of ethology.* New York: Springer-Verlag.

Luthans, F. (1995). *Organizational behavior* (7th ed.). New York: Free Press.

Lykken, D.T. (1995). *The antisocial personalities*. Hillsdale, NJ: Lawrence Erlbaum.

Mailer, N. (1957). The white negro (superficial reflections on the hipster). *Dissent Magazine*, Summer.

Maner, J.K., DeWall, C.N., Baumeister, R.F., & Schaller, M. (2007). Does social exclusion motivate interpersonal reconnection? Resolving the "Porcupine Problem." *Journal of Personality and Social Psychology, 92*(1), 42–55.

Marcuse, H. (1964). *One dimensional man*. Boston, MA: Beacon Press.

Markham, U. (1993). *How to deal with difficult people*. London, UK: Thorsons.

Marx, K. (1964). *The social and economic manuscripts of 1844*. New York: International Publishers.

Masri, A. (1984). *The hydraulic principle and the victimization of civilians during the Lebanese civil war*. (Unpublished master's thesis). Lebanese University, Beirut, Lebanon.

Menninger, K. (1938). *Man against himself*. New York: Free Press.

Merton, R.K. (1968). *Social theory and social structure*. New York: Free Press.

Miller, N., Pedersen W.C., Earleywine, M., & Pollock, V.E. (2003). A theoretical model of triggered displaced aggression. *Personality and Social Psychology Review, 7*(1), 75–97.

Mitchell, M. (2009). *Complexity: A guided tour*. Oxford, UK: Oxford University Press.

Mummendy, A., Linneweber, V., & Löschper, G. (1984). Aggression: From act to interaction. In A. Mummendy (Ed.), *Social psychology of aggression: From individual behavior to social interaction* (pp. 69–106). New York: Springer.

Neuman, J.H., & Baron, R.A. (1996). Workplace violence and workplace aggression: Evidence on their relative frequency and potential causes. *Aggressive Behavior, 22*(3), 161–73.

Neuman, J.H., & Baron, R.A. (1997). Aggression in the workplace. In R. Giacalone & J. Greenberg (Eds.), *Antisocial behaviour in organizations* (pp. 37–67). Thousand Oaks, CA: Sage.

Nietzsche, F.W. (1967). *Beyond good and evil: Prelude to a philosophy of the future*. London: Allen & Unwin. (Original work published 1886).

Nietzsche, F.W. (1968). *Joyful wisdom*. New York: Frederick Unger. (Original work published 1882).

Novaco, R.W. (1976). The functions and regulation of the arousal of anger. *American Journal of Psychiatry, 133*(10), 1124–28.

Obeid, A. (1999). Personal communication.

Parsons, T. (1951). *The social system*. New York: Free Press.

Perrow, C. (1979). *Complex organizations: A critical essay*. Glenview, IL: Scott Foresman.

Peter, L.J., & Hull, R. (1970). *The Peter principle*. New York: Marrow.

Peters, T.J., & Waterman, R.H. (1982). *In search of excellence: Lessons from America's best-run companies*. New York: Harper & Row.

Rassy, S. (1976). *Village talk and city talk*. Beirut: Noufal Press.

Robbins, S.P. (1985). *Organizational theory*. Englewood Cliffs, NJ: Prentice Hall.

Robinson, S.L., & Bennett, R.J. (1995). A typology of deviant workplace behaviors: A multidimensional scaling study. *Academy of Management Journal, 38*(2), 555–72.

Robinson, S.L., & Schabram, K. (2017). Invisible work: Workplace ostracism as aggression. In N.A. Bowling & M.S. Hershcovis (Eds.), *Research and theory on workplace aggression* (pp. 221–44). Cambridge, UK: Cambridge University Press.

Ross, R.R. (1999). *Interpersonal sabotage: How to survive in organizations* (Conference paper). Ottawa, ON: Cognitive Centre of Canada.

Rue, L. (1994). *By the grace of guile: The role of deception in natural history and human affairs*. New York: Oxford University Press.

Sankar, Y. (1994). *Organizational behaviour: The ethical challenge*. Toronto, ON: Canadian Scholars Press.

Sellin, T. (1938). Culture conflict and crime. *Social Science Research Council Bulletin, 41*, 63–70.

Selye, H. (1956). *The stress of life*. New York: McGraw-Hill.

Simonton, O.C. (1978). *Getting well again*. Los Angeles, CA: Tracher

Sorel, G. (1972). *Réflexions sur la violence*. Paris: M. Rivière. (Original work published in 1908).

Sternberg, R.J. (2005). Foolishness. In R.J. Sternberg & J. Jordan (Eds.), *A handbook of wisdom: Psychological perspectives* (pp. 331–52). New York: Cambridge University Press.

Stone, M.H. (1993). *Abnormalities of personality: Within and beyond the realm of treatment*. New York: W.W. Norton & Company.

Sutherland, E.H. (1947). *The principles of criminology* (4th ed.). Philadelphia: Lippincott.

Taleb, N.N. (2012). *Antifragile: Things that gain from disorder*. New York: Random House.

Tedeschi, J.T. & Felson, R.B. (Eds). (1993). *Aggression and violence: A social interactionist perspective*. Washington, DC: American Psychological Association.

Tedeschi, J.T. & Felson, R.B. (Eds). (1994). *Violence, aggression and, coercive actions*. Washington, DC: American Psychological Association.

Tedeschi, J.T., & Norman, N. (1985). Social mechanisms of displaced aggression. In E.J. Lawler (Ed.), *Advances in group processes: Theory and research* (vol. 2, pp. 29–56). Greenwich, CT: JAI.

Thompson, V.A. (1961). *Modern organization*. New York: A. Knopf.

Thorngate, W. (1990). The economy of attention and the development of psychology. *Canadian Psychology/ Psychologie canadienne, 31*(3), 262–71.

Tobak, M. (1989). Lying and the paranoid personality. (Letter to the editor). *American Journal of Psychiatry, 146*, 125–26.

Twale, D.J., & De Luca, B.M. (2008). *Faculty incivility: The rise of the academic bully culture and what to do about it*. San Francisco, CA: Jossey-Bass.

Van Soest, D. (1997). *The global crisis of violence: Common problems, universal causes, shared solutions*. Annapolis, MD: NASW Press.

Velasquez, M.G. (1982). *Business ethics: Concepts and cases*. Englewood Cliffs, NJ: Prentice Hall.

Weber, M. (1947). *The theory of social and economic organizations*. New York: Free Press.

Wheeler, S., & Rothman, M.L. (1982). The organization as weapon in white collar crime. *Michigan Law Review, 80*(7), 1403–26.

Williams, R. (2011). The silent epidemic: Workplace bullying. *Psychology Today, 3*, 5.

Wolman, B.B. (1973). *Dictionary of behavioral science*. New York: Van Nostrand.

Wrong, D.H. (1961). The oversocialized conception of man. *American Sociological Review, 26*(2), 183–93.

INDEX

academic incivility, 51

affect withdrawal, 152–53

aggression

    challenge of reducing, 137–38

    definitions of, ix, 2–3

    effect of surplus on organizations, 168

    and entropy, 169–70

    expressed through inaction, 7

    forms of, 3–4

    as fundamental part of human interaction, 137

    inhibition of in humans, 42–43

    K. Lorenz's view of, 70–71

    measurement of, 17

    spread of, 170

    suppression of and guilt, 78–79

    as term used interchangeably with violence, 1–2. *See also* confrontational aggression; non-confrontational aggression; workplace aggression

alienation, 9–10, 119–20

anger/rage

    avoidance of dealing with, 35, 59, 61

    displacing, 22–23, 64, 134

    its role in confrontational v. non-confrontational aggression, 13

    masking of, 13, 35, 70, 114

    misdirecting of, 72

    and paranoid personality disorder, 89

    as result of hydraulic expression of aggression, 74

    and sabotage, 21

    suppression of, 9–10

anomie, 120–21

anti-organizational personality profile, 107–10

anti-social aggression, 34–36

antisocial personality disorder, 95–99

anxiety

    and neurotic disorders, 152

over job security, 68
and personality disorders, 85, 86
and regression of ethics, 44, 45,
47
Arab society, 59, 69, 102, 107, 123–25
assertiveness, 133
attention withdrawal, 62–64
avoidant personality disorder, 101,
155

backstabbing, 60, 74
biased punctuation of conflict, 156
bimodal theory of aggression
and bimodal shifts, 15, 70, 145
and dialectical relationship
between confrontational
and non-confrontational
aggression, x
importance of balance in, 14–15,
159–60, 164, 167–68
incorporating within
organizations, 158–60
and masking of aggression, ix
borderline personality disorder, 101
bullying, xi–xii
bureaucracies
of Arab countries, 123–25
camouflaged behaviour in, 45–48
and ethical regression, 43–48
and hiring people with
personality disorders, 83,
160–62
how they've taken over
management of conflict, 8–11
narcissism in, 159

and pathological narcissism,
122–23
permeating all aspect of modern
life, 33–34
pros and cons of, 29–30
role in use of camouflaged
aggression, 24–25, 31–32,
37–41
sabotage by, 24–25, 60
sense of power within, 157–58
strategy for dealing with
personality disorders within,
115–16
as system of organization, 27–28
techniques of camouflaged
aggression used by, 55–70
and use of deceit, 131, 132
bureaupathology, 29

camouflage behaviour, ix–x, 36–37,
42, 45–48
camouflaged aggression
in animals, 36–37
as anti-social behaviour, 35–36
in Arab countries, 102, 123–25
balanced with confrontational
aggression at conceptual level,
140–44
bureaucracies role in, 24–25,
31–32, 37–41
as cause of entropy, 169–70, 171
characteristics of, 35, 37
cognitive strategy to combat,
163–65
as complex society, 169, 171
and cross-cultural values, 123–25

and displacement, 22–23, 25

effects of on workplace, 8–10

effects on victims' health, 114–15,
121

expressed as regressive
aggression, 76–77

expressed as revenge, 129

how it increases aggression
overall, 79, 138

how it's learned, 121–22

impact of personality disorders
on, 82–83, 88–90, 103, 128,
153–54

importance of theoretical
understanding of, xv, 28, 164

importation of, 124–25

ineffectiveness of ethicality as
strategy to fight, 162–63

and institutionalized hypocrisy,
131, 133–34

modal imbalance favours, 167–68

non-confrontational nature of,
10–11

and pathological narcissism,
122–23

in political movements, 113

possible addictive nature of,
113–14

and power games, 51–53, 119–20

seeking the point of least
resistance, 73–76

as self-destructiveness, 77–78

serious consequences for society
in, 41, 170–71

and social media, 9

steps for reducing in
organizations, 144–51

techniques of, 55–70

and technology, 9, 32, 33, 64–65

through human evolution, 39–40.
See also non-confrontational
aggression

carpet pulling, 146

casualness, 151

charisma, 67, 162

civility, 50–51, 150–51

Cleckley, Harvey, 85, 95, 98

complex systems, 32–33, 168

conflict avoidance syndrome,
103–06, 127–28, 160–62

conflict reconciliation as personality
profile, 106–07, 161

confrontational aggression
in balance with non-
confrontational aggression,
14–15

balancing with camouflaged
aggression at conceptual level,
140–44

balancing with camouflaged
aggression at practical level,
144–51

celebrated and idealized, 40

characterized as violence, 125–28

dialectical relationship with non-
confrontational aggression, x

eight value assumptions about,
125–36

exaggerated idea of consequences
of, 24

explained, 4–5

how it differs from non-
  confrontational aggression,
  11–13, 16, 70
management of in workplace,
  17–21
and pseudo-confrontation,
  132–33
and retaliation, 23–24, 128–30
values of, 164
conspiracies, 50, 156–57
conspiratorial thinking, 102
convergence on injustice, 50
corruption, 32–33

deceit/deception, 131–32
decision laundering, 146, 148
delaying decisions, 58–61
denial of problems, 115, 157
dignity
  as abstract construction of self,
    129
  attacks on, 50
  and avoiding poorly managed
    agencies, 116
  as part of cognitive strategy
    to combat camouflaged
    aggression, 164–65
  as prosocial value, 143–44
displacement
  described, 18
  effect on health of victims, 114
  from forgiveness, 130
  as major facet of camouflaged
    aggression, 21–23, 72
  and resonance, 25
  as self-destructiveness, 77

upwards, 24
dissipation, 20
dusting, 146

economy of the self, 116
ego bashing, 68–69, 112
entrapment, 66
entropy, 169–70, 171
equivalence, principle of, 94–95
ethical consciousness, 74, 162–63
ethicality, compromised, 109–10,
  162–63
ethical regression, 43–50, 50–51
exaggerated perception of
  conspiracy, 156
explosion/explosive violence, 20,
  170, 171

false accusations, 156–57
fatigue, 20
fear of success, 153
firing, 61, 62
flattening effect of hierarchical
  structures, 31, 33, 65
forgiveness, 20, 130
formalization, 32, 123
freezing, 56
Freud, Sigmund, 71, 78, 93, 132

getting even revenge, 130
good manners/civility, 50–51, 150–51
gossip, 7, 9, 11, 60
Grover, Chander P., 158
guilt, 78–79, 96, 109

Harrington, Alan, 98
health of aggressed victims, 26,
    114–15, 121
heating up and cooling down model,
    19–20
hidden agendas, 149–50
histrionic personality disorder, 99,
    155
homologies, 42
honour
    as abstract value leading to
        confrontation, 123–24, 129
    as part of cognitive strategy
        to combat camouflaged
        aggression, 164–65
    as prosocial value, 143–44
    used as policing agency, 142
hydraulic models of aggression
    examples of, 72–73
    leading to chaos and entropy, 170
    main assumptions of, 71–72
    in organizations, 73–76
    and self-destructiveness, 77–78
hydraulic victimization, 146

inaccessability, 64–65
indecision, 55–56
information as weapon, 38, 59–62
institutionalization of anti-charisma,
    162
institutionalized hypocrisy, 133–34
intellectual skills, 108–09, 132
interdependence, 33–34
interpersonal sabotage, 7

javelin in sack story, 135–36

Kernberg, Otto, 91–92
kindness, extravagant, 66–67

labelling behaviour, 145–46
leadership, 171
Lebanese Civil War, 72–73
legal process, 8–9
Lorenz, Konrad, 4, 42, 49, 70–71

Machiavellian power tactics, 52–53,
    73, 98, 102
Mailer, Norman, 97–98
malignant aggression, 76–77, 120–21,
    146
malignant narcissism, 91–92
managerial wisdom, 138–39
Marxist political groups in Lebanon,
    102
The Mask of Sanity (Cleckley), 85,
    95, 98
mass media, 9
mental games, 113
minimal self, 134–36, 161
mobbing, xi, 49–50
modal shifts, 15, 70, 145
moral callousness, 48
moral segmentation, 48
Al-Mutanabbi, 8

narcissism
    and anti-organizational
        personality, 107
    within bureaucracies, 159

as central to all personality
disorders, 101–02
dealing with in organizations,
154, 155
and deceit, 131
and ego bashing, 69
features of, 90–95
healthy, 165
malignant, 91–92
pathological, 101, 113, 122–23,
129
and technology, 65
National Research Council of
Canada (NRC), 158
negative feedback, 78, 79
neurotic disorders, 85, 87, 152–54
Nietzsche, Frederick, xiv, 116, 130
non-confrontational aggression
acts in balance with
confrontational aggression,
14–15
allowing for retaliation after, 23
dialectical relationship with
confrontational aggression, x
examples of, 6–7
explained, 5–6
how it differs from
confrontational aggression,
11–13, 16, 70
main approaches used to study in
workplace, x–xii
management of in workplace,
17–21
and phylogenetic regression, 70
as self-destructiveness, 77
use of camouflage in, 10–11

and warehousing, 25–26. *See also*
camouflaged aggression
non-interference, 65

obsessive-compulsive personality
disorder, 100, 113–14, 155
organizational foliage, 146
organizations
achieving modal balance in,
158–60
anti-social aggression in, 34–36
balancing confrontational and
camouflaged aggression at
conceptual level, 140–44
bureaucracies as source for
aggression in, 37–39
as complex systems, 32–33
dealing with personality disorders
in, 151–55
effect of personalities on, 81,
82–83, 84, 87
effect of personality disorders on,
87–103, 105–10
ethical regression in, 43–49, 50
formalization of, 32
and framework of managerial
wisdom for, 138–39
how bureaucracies work in,
27–30
how to deal with refutation of
blame, 155–57
hydraulic models of aggression in,
72, 73–76
interdependence of, 33–34
and malignant aggression,
120–21

manner of getting revenge in, 129–30

modifications to structure of, 31–32

and negative feedback, 78, 79

and neutralization of conflict by hypocrisy in, 133–34

personality disorders in political, 112–13

personality disorders in voluntary, 110–11

porcupine effect from, 115–16

and power games, 51–53

and self-destructiveness, 77–78

steps to reduce camouflaged aggression in, 144–51

using a balance sheet to assess personality disorders, 116–17. *See also* bureaucracies; workplace aggression

ostracism, 63–64

overwork, 62

paranoid personality disorder, 88–90, 102, 156–57

paranoid thinking, 135

passive aggression

dealing with in organizations, 154

examples of, 6–7

explained, 6

features of, 87–88

how it adapts to organizations, 83

by neurotics, 152–53

potential normalizing of, 128

use of technology in, 8

pathological narcissism, 101, 113, 122–23, 129

personalistic attributions, 156

personality disorders

balance sheet accounting of, 116–17

cause of, 82

dealing with in organizations, 154–55

defined, 85

and displaced aggression, 25

effect on bureaucracies, 115–16

effect on organizations, 81, 82–83, 84, 87

features of, 86

lack of research on, 85

in political organizations, 112–13

types of, 87–101

in voluntary organizations, 110–11

personality-job fit theory, 82–83

personality profiles, 103–10

Peter Principle, 152

phylogenetic regression, 42–43, 45–48, 49, 70

policy restrictions or following established procedure, 58

political organizations, 112–13

porcupine effect, 115, 116

position victimology, 146

position vulnerability, 146

power, 157–58. *See also* Machiavellian power tactics

power games, 51–53, 67, 114, 119–20

pragmatism, 43–48

pseudo-confrontation, 132–33

psychiatric disorders, 84–85

psychopathy
    categories of, 84–85
    dealing with in organizations,
        154–55
    and deceit, 132
    effect on organizations, 97–99
    features of, 95–97
    research into, 85
psychosocial perspective, 82–83

rage. *See* anger/rage
random murder, 76
Rassy, Salam, 135
regression
    and camouflage strategy, ix–x, 24
    ethical, 43–49
    phylogenetic, 41–43
regressive aggression, 76–77
religious duty, 50
resonance, 25
retaliation, 23–24, 128–30, 156–57
retributive vengeance, 129
rigidity, 56–57
rumour mongering, 60

sabotage, 7, 21, 24, 60, 122–23
schizoid personality disorder, 101
schizotypal personality disorder, 101
security, undermining, 68
self-destructiveness, 77–78, 153–54
sexualization, 67
sickness of aggressed victims, 26,
    114–15, 121
situational vulnerability, 75–76
social alienation, 119–20
social exchange theory, 67

social learning theory, 121
social media, 9
sociobiological deterioration, 171
splitting mechanism, 93–94
status inconsistency, 69
structural sociology theory, 81
survivalist mentality, 135–36

technology
    and complexity, 32–34
    as means of camouflaged
        aggression, 9, 64–65
    and modifications to bureaucracy,
        31
    and organizational unhappiness,
        78
    use of in passive aggression, 8
termination of employment, 61, 62
third parties, 7
time manipulation, 57–59, 62

vendettas, 69–70
venting, 19–20
victimology of positions, 75–76
victims
    effect of aggression on health of,
        114–15, 121
    how to deal with innocent,
        156–57
    indentification of, 146–47
    popularity of the role of, 135, 136
violence, 1–2, 23, 125–27
voicemail, 64–65
voluntary organizations, 110–11

waiting, prolonged, 59

warehousing, 26

workplace aggression
  allowing managed retaliation for,
    23–24
  and anti-social behaviour, 34–36
  and avoidant personality disorder,
    101
  classification of, 28
  cognitive approach to
    management of, xv–xvi
  and displacement, 21–23, 24, 25
  effect of increased research into, 2
  and histrionic personality
    disorder, 99
  how it becomes camouflaged,
    8–10
  how it differs from societal
    aggression, ix

and incivility, 50–51
main approaches used to study,
  x–xii
management of, 17–21
and mobbing, 50
mode as central variable in, 4
and power games, 51–53
research on, xii–xiv, 138–39
as result of societal anomie,
  120–21
using modal shifts to control, 15
and warehousing, 26
and zero tolerance for violence,
  126. *See also* camouflaged
  aggression; confrontational
  aggression

yo-yoing, 146

Other Titles from University of Alberta Press

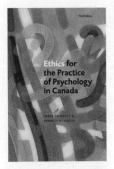

Ethics for the Practice of Psychology in Canada
Third Edition

DEREK TRUSCOTT & KENNETH H. CROOK

This textbook outlines what is expected of Canadian psychologists and how to practice ethically.

Driven to Kill
Vehicles as Weapons

J. PETER ROTHE

Rothe examines the use of vehicles for assault, abduction, rape, terrorism, suicide, and murder.

Overcoming Conflicting Loyalties
Intimate Partner Violence, Community Resources, and Faith

IRENE SEVCIK, MICHAEL ROTHERY,
NANCY NASON-CLARK & ROBERT PYNN

Benefits of secular and sacral communities working together to help victims of intimate partner violence.

More information at uap.ualberta.ca